PSYCHO BUSTERS

THE NOVEL

Illustrations by Rando Ayamine
Translated by Katy Bridges

BALLANTINE BOOKS NEW YORK

Book 1

PSYCHO BUSTERS

THE NOVEL

YUYA AOKI

A Del Rey Manga/Kodansha Trade Paperback Original

Psycho Busters: Book One copyright © 2004 by Yuya Aoki
English translation copyright © 2008 by Yuya Aoki

Published in the United States by Del Rey Books, an imprint of The Random House Publishing Group, a division of Random House, Inc., New York.

DEL REY is a registered trademark and the Del Rey colophon is a trademark of Random House, Inc.

Publication rights arranged through Kodansha Ltd.

First published in Japan in 2004 by Kodansha Ltd., Tokyo, as *Saikobasutaazu 1*.

Library of Congress Cataloging-in-Publication Data
Aoki, Yuya.
(Saiko basutazu. English)
Psycho busters : the novel / Yuya Aoki ; illustrations by Rando Ayamine ; translated by Katy Bridges.
p.   cm.
ISBN-13: 978-0-345-49882-3 (v. 1 : pbk.)
I. Ayamine, Rando.   II. Bridges, Katy.   III. Title.
PL867.5.O43S25 2008
895.6'36—dc22   2007043846

Printed in the United States of America

www.delreymanga.com

9 8 7 6 5 4 3 2 1

Translator: Katy Bridges
Cover illustration: Rando Ayamine
Text design: Karin Batten

CONTENTS

ILLUSTRATIONS

From far away came the barking of dogs.

It was nothing like the baying of wild dogs. It sounded strangely organized, as if the dogs were in pursuit of prey. They sounded like hunting dogs. However, it was almost midnight, an hour at which few hunters venture out.

But the dogs' prey was not an animal. It was human.

Crunch crunch crunch.

Leaves crackled underfoot, and the sound rushed through the darkness. Four shadows dashed down the opposite slope of the valley, as quickly as a herd of wild stags. As they ran, they threaded through the trees easily, even though it was dark and there was no moonlight to guide them. The forest was full of shadows, and the spreading branches of the conifer trees blocked out the sky. The darkness made it hard to see even where to step.

And still they kept up their pace, only because of their leader.

The boy's guidance was unerring. Just as bats use sonar to fly in total darkness, he did not rely on his vision to move through the shadows. But he was not exactly using sonar. The sense that guided him was supernatural. And it was because of this power that he and his friends were now fugitives.

Just then, the four friends reached a mountain stream running through the woods.

"Kaito, Ayano, Xiao Long!"

The leader stopped abruptly. "We can't go right or left. There are Farmers ahead. One, two . . . no, six of them. And they're also behind us and getting closer all the time. We're completely surrounded!"

"Hah, six of them is nothing, Jôi. I'll burn them out myself."

A tall boy brushed Jôi aside to stand at the head of the group. Then he looked all around, gritting his teeth, as if he could attack and kill his enemies with the force of his hatred alone.

And, as if responding to his hatred, the leaves on the ground began to smolder.

Like his friend Jôi, the tall boy also had a talent that was hard to explain.

"Kaito, stop!" A girl with long hair grabbed the tall boy's arm. "You must not kill. Not even Farmers."

Her right and left eyes were two different colors. The right was a profoundly gloomy brown, but the left was clear and blue. She liked to think she'd gotten her left eye from her Japanese mother and her right from her German father.

She also liked to think that her unusual powers had something to do with her strange eyes.

"But Ayano, they'll take us back to the Greenhouse. I mean, do you think we'll ever get another chance to escape?"

"Wait. This is not the time to argue about this." The boy who interrupted was a couple of years younger than the others. He had an unusual accent, an inheritance from his Chinese father.

"Let's ask Jôi. He *knows*."

"Xiao Long is right. Shall we do it?" Ayano pressed Kaito to agree with her.

"Well, what do you say, Jôi?"

Averting his eyes, Jôi murmured, as if he found it hard to speak. "We have to jump. Into that mountain stream."

They looked down into the valley. The river was thirty feet below.

"Are you serious? Can you promise that we'll survive?" Kaito grabbed Jôi by the collar.

"Relax, Kaito. No one's going to die. I promise."

"We've got to trust Jôi. I mean, he's gotten us this far."

At Xiao Long's words, Kaito let go of Jôi. "Fine. Still, if I get hurt badly and I'm dying, you better save me, Xiao Long. You can do that, can't you?"

Healing was Xiao Long's power.

"They're coming. They've made it to the other side of the thicket." Jôi lowered his voice.

"Somebody else go first!" Kaito blurted. He was so impatient he raised his voice. In answer, one of the pursuing dogs began to bark.

"Me, of course." Jôi edged toward the cliff. "Before I jump, everybody listen close."

"Kaito"

"Huh?"

"Ayano, Xiao Long."

"What?"

"What is it, Jôi?"

"If we survive, the first thing we do is look for Kakeru."

"Kakeru? Who's that?" asked Ayano.

"I don't know, either. I only know that . . . Kakeru is one of us."

"Hurry up! They're coming!"

"Quickly! Do it! The enemy's coming!"

As if Kaito's words had physically pushed him, Jôi leaned forward over the edge of the precipice. Then Jôi disappeared into the river, leaving the other three on the cliff top.

As if he were competing with Jôi, Kaito threw himself off right after. Next went Ayano, and, just as Xiao Long jumped, men with guns and dogs emerged from the bushes.

"They jumped!" someone yelled. A shot rang out. It made a dull *thud* that sounded somehow moist, quite unlike the dry *crack* of a bullet.

Searchlights shone down on the river's surface. But the four friends had already disappeared, swallowed by the swiftly moving current.

"We lost them."

"There's no way they survived a jump like that." The speaker sounded resigned.

Only one man, the group's apparent leader, seemed to disagree. He stared down at the river for some time. Then he clicked his tongue and said confidently, "They've got Jôi with them. He wouldn't jump in there knowing he was going to die."

"What do you mean, Director Ikushima?"

Ikushima looked away. "Nothing . . ." he mumbled. He'd almost blown it. No one must know Jôi's secret. No one must find out the truth about the boy, not even the director of the Greenhouse or even the members of the Masquerade . . .

"Just find them!" commanded Ikushima harshly, so that his subordinates wouldn't see how shaken he was. "Don't let them get away! Especially Jôi!"

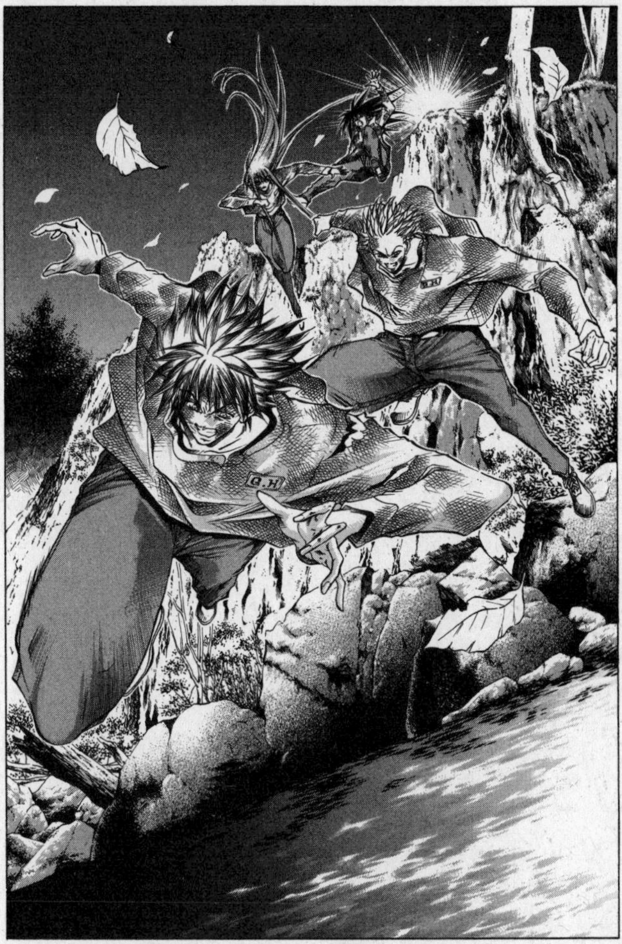
G.H

PSYCHO BUSTERS

THE NOVEL

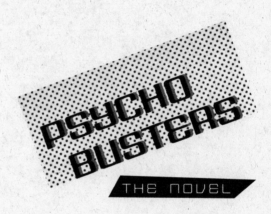

THE GHOST GIRL

Deep in the forest, the trees were several hundred years old, and so large that they looked like pillars for the ceiling of the sky. And in this forest was heard a terrible sound, like the ground rumbling. A swirl of fierce energy was coming toward me.

It was a spell cast by the six Evil Mages who had surrounded me.

"Warrior of legend. Now there is no escape."

This was the Evil Mage who was wearing a hideous flesh mask. He looked at me and grinned. A "flesh mask" is a cursed mask made from the face of a murdered man. This mask becomes a part of the face of its wearer. In time, it would drain all human feeling out of its wearer and, in exchange, grant amazing magical powers. Evil Mages were willing to make such bargains with the devil if it meant gaining the power to do whatever they wished.

I was facing my death. But worried about the trembling princess clinging to me, I fought my fear and laughed boldly.

"It's all right. You're with me. I'll beat them back with my dragon sword!" I raised my sword above my head.

Now I was a warrior. I was a holy knight who had been given an ancient sword with which I would defeat the Evil Mages and save the princess. Every fiber of my being was prepared for battle.

My sword got its power from the forest and could repel evil magic. The forest's power began to pour into me. After the battle, what waited for me: peace and prosperity, or frustration and despair?

I gathered all my power into the sword and called down the thunder. The thunder roared and brilliant light simultaneously lit up every dark nook and corner of the forest.

The final battle had begun.

"Still at it, Kakeru?" My oldest sister's laughter snatched me back to the real world.

"It's silly to play with dolls and talk to yourself! Especially when you're in the *ninth grade*." This was my youngest sister, who was in her second year of high school.

When my oldest sister said, "And the skanky clothes you put on those girl dolls. Gross!" in a voice so loud the neighbors could hear, my next oldest sister added gleefully, "Are you kidding?! Ooh, yuck, you're not doing kinky stuff in the middle of the night with those dolls, are you?!" They were exploiting the situation like a couple of gangsters trying to extort money. Then they tried to snatch the figures away.

I quickly put them away in my desk—the holy knight figurine, which I guess you could say did look a little like me, and the princess in her dress, which I have to admit *was* a little revealing.

"Shut up! You can't just barge into people's rooms

whenever you want!" I didn't have time to hide the six Evil Mages. They stood idly on top of my small study desk, in a circle, like they were playing duck, duck goose.

My mother grabbed one. "Kakeru! It's dinnertime! How many times do I have to call you? And I didn't know you were still playing with dolls! Don't you think it's time for you to grow up? You have your high school entrance exams next year!" She just kept going on and on.

"Yeah, I know!"

I stood up and turned off the lights, hoping it would encourage my mother and sisters to leave.

They weren't dolls. They were figurines, now a world-class fine art in Japan. And I wasn't *playing*. I was creating an original fantasy world. I didn't want them thinking they were just plastic toys. These were my own original characters that I had fashioned myself out of model-making material. But these people just didn't get it.

When I got downstairs, it smelled like onions everywhere. Mom had put onions in the curry again. I *hate* onions. Why couldn't she just cut me a break, just this once? Why, even though I asked her every time not to put any in? Why couldn't she just listen to me? The smell of raw onions makes me want to throw up. And cooked onions are too sweet, have a weird texture, and are impossible to swallow.

"Ooohh, smells good, doesn't it, Kakeru. Lots of onions," the younger of my two older sisters said, flaring her nostrils. She knew I hated onions and said it on purpose to upset me.

My oldest sister couldn't resist making the same dig. "Oh, wow, all those onions make it look so good," she said, laughing to herself and clapping her hands.

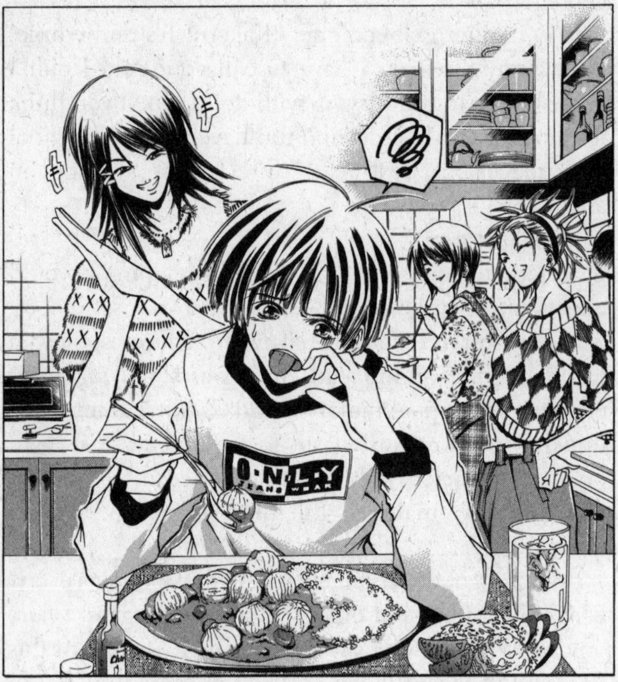
O·N·L·Y
JEANS WEAR

"I always ask you not to put onions in," I complained as I sat down at the dinner table.

But my mother said, just as if she had not heard me, "This curry is sweet and delicious. It's got lots of onions in it. Onions clean out your circulatory system. They're so good for you." And then she served me some, from a ladle heaped with onions.

I sighed. Did these people hate me or something? I wasn't a good student like my oldest sister, who had gone on to a famous university, and it wasn't like I was as good at sports as the youngest of my sisters, who was on the gymnastics team at school. I had already disappointed my parents' expectations when I'd failed to get into private school for junior high, so now I was going to a neighborhood public school that didn't have that great a reputation. And since I'm always getting beat up and bullied, my mom doesn't think all that much of me. People say that I'm willful because I'm the baby of the family. Of course, I was only claiming rights that were naturally mine, but my mom and my older sisters say it was just selfishness.

But I do have one good thing going for me, even if it sounds bad to say it about myself. I'm pretty good-looking. I have a nice face. I think I have features like an idol in one of those Johnny and the Associates–style boy bands. My sisters all have narrow eyes like Mom, but I have double-lidded eyes like my dad.

Maybe that's why he'd always had a soft spot for me when I was little. I was so happy back then. He bought me all the modeling materials I wanted, and he always praised the figurines I made. But then, one year ago, everything changed when he was sent to his company's branch office in Kyushu—without his family. Now, surrounded by my mother and older sisters, I feel like I'm being pressed in on all sides. At first I resisted, but with each of them talking three times as much as I do, and since three times three equals nine, nine against one was no contest.

My dad and I have the same taste in food, so now meals were never anything I wanted to eat. It was always what my onion-loving mother and older sisters wanted. If I was watching anime on TV, one of my sisters soon came and switched it to one of those meaningless variety shows. My room had no lock on the door, and before I knew it, my mother's and sister's clothes were hanging all over the place. Even worse, my mom had taken over one of the drawers in the built-in dresser in my room.

There was no place for me. Not one place in this house I could call my own, where I could relax completely.

It wasn't like school was a refuge for me, either. Especially because I'd gone into a new class when I went into ninth grade, and hadn't really gotten close to anyone. Of the forty students in my class, three were your classic burnout type who almost never came to school, ten were the kind of halfhearted delinquents who dyed their hair weird colors and snuck off to smoke cigarettes, and five were bookworms who always had their cram-school textbooks open during lessons or lunch break. The remaining twenty were just perfectly average. It'd been almost one month since the new school year started and I could hardly remember their names.

Also, my friends from my class the year before started studying hard for high school entrance exams the moment they became ninth graders, and were somehow distant, even when I saw them at school. *Yeah, we don't have time to just hang out and play.* When I noticed they felt that way, I started distancing myself from them.

"Kakeru, are you listening to me?" said my mother, setting a cup of water violently down in front of me.

"Huh? What?"

"See? You weren't listening, were you? I knew it." My sister was making fun of me again.

"What, Mom? What were you talking about?" I said.

My mother said dejectedly, "It's okay. You can make dinner yourself."

I'd been helping her make dinner a lot of nights for a good reason: Golden Week, a whole week of vacation, started the next day, and I would be staying by myself at the house. I'd decided two weeks ago. When I had heard that Dad was going on a business trip overseas, and he couldn't go to Hawaii with us, I figured the whole trip was off, but naturally my sisters stubbornly insisted right in front of me that we could go without Dad. Gradually my mother got excited about it, too.

Heaven forbid. Going to Hawaii without Dad would be no fun at all. I'm not the greatest swimmer, and unlike my sisters, I had no desire to go shopping for fancy stuff from designer stores. It'd be like our trip last summer to Guam all over again, when my mom and sisters wore me out dragging me to duty-free shops while my dad played golf. If Dad wasn't going, then I wasn't going—and when I said this, my mom and two sisters looked thrilled.

Yes. Rebellion! I would use this chance to show them I could stand up for myself, too.

Besides, wouldn't it be a wonderful thing to be by myself for a week! A peaceful week when I could do whatever I wanted, without my mom's constant criticism, or my sisters' boasting and sarcastic remarks. It had to be way better than a trip to Hawaii. I had made the right choice.

"Thanks for dinner," I said abruptly, getting up from the table.

She looked at the mountain of onion pieces I'd made a great show of leaving on my plate and glared at me. She cleared away my plate roughly, making a loud clunk.

"You didn't eat your onions again. When I see things like this, it makes me wonder if you really are going to be all right while we're away."

"Leave him alone, Mom. He's old enough to take care of himself. He's in ninth grade, after all," said the younger of my older sisters.

"True . . . Oh, no! If we don't leave soon, we'll be late. We fly out of Narita at ten, which means we need to be there by eight-thirty." It seemed like my oldest sister was on her way to Hawaii already. She'd been gazing at pamphlets of Hawaiian tours all through dinner and had left more than half of the curry rice she loved so much on her plate.

Just after I helped Mom clean up after dinner, the taxi they had ordered arrived outside the house, almost as if it had been waiting for them to finish.

"Bye, Kakeru. We'll be back soon. Finish the rest of the cleaning up and be good, will you?"

"I said I would. Have a good time."

I smiled, feeling footloose and fancy free, but also a little lonely, as I sent the three of them off with an exaggerated wave.

As dusk fell, Xiao Long and Ayano were nearly at their limit. They were carrying Jôi through the forest, which was muddy from days of rain.

They'd had nothing to eat for the last two days but some chocolate and biscuits they'd managed to conceal in their pockets, and nothing to drink but river water. Their flight from the Farmers had been hard on them emotionally and physically.

And above all, if they couldn't let the seriously injured Jôi rest someplace warm, his wounds could prove fatal.

"Ayano, we've got to get Jôi somewhere where he can rest."

Xiao Long was completely worn out as he said this. He'd exhausted his chi to treat Jôi's injury. Now he was so tired he could barely stand.

"You're right. We've got to do something."

But the Farmers knew they'd floated downstream by grabbing onto pieces of driftwood, and most of all, the enemy was a handpicked elite of very capable people led by Arata Ikushima. They were also equipped with a handheld machine to detect Ayano's and Xiao Long's brain waves.

If they chose their camping spot carelessly, then they might be captured before they had time to fight the approaching Farmers.

"Ayano! We've got trouble! Jôi's heartbeat is stopping!" Xiao Long exclaimed. He put his head to Jôi's chest.

"Huh? What'll we do?!"

Was there a cave where they could find shelter? In desperation they looked around where they were. Then a place where the trees became sparse came into sight. The red evening sun hit their eyes, reflecting off something.

They strained their eyes.

A glass window.

"There's a cabin! Let's rest there for now!" Eagerly they set out for the shack, forcing their feet, which felt as heavy as lead, to move, as they supported Jôi's limp form. They opened the rotten door, entered the cabin, and then collapsed on the floor. Chests heaving from exhaustion, they looked around the cabin. There were piles of old newspapers everywhere.

"There's newspaper. We can use the paper like a blanket to keep him warm." Xiao Long happily gathered up the papers and spread them over Jôi's sleeping form.

"I'll send Jôi some chi to restore his heart. Could you look for a place that's a little warmer and safer while I do that, Ayano?"

Almost before the words had left his mouth, Xiao Long put his left hand on Jôi's chest and shut his eyes and began the deep *qigong* breathing. "Kohhhh . . ."

Ayano, whose eyes were more sensitive than the average person's, saw the flow of chi that Xiao Long was sending to Jôi. To Ayano, it looked like a torrent of rushing light. It spiraled clockwise slowly as it streamed into Jôi's body.

With each deep breath, the chi flowed toward Jôi, and life gradually returned to his purple face.

But they had to be vigilant. If they laid him down to rest in a place as damp and cold as this, surely he would soon again be in danger.

What Jôi had said before they'd jumped into the river came back to Ayano.

Find Kakeru.

Surely that had been what he'd said.

"Keep going, Xiao Long. I'm going to go look." But just after she said this, Ayano only sat down in a corner of the shack, took a deep breath, and shut both her eyes.

That night I hit the sack at a little after eight. I did that because I'd eaten dinner at five-something, and if I stayed up late I'd just get hungry again. And last night I'd been so excited thinking about today that I couldn't sleep and stayed up till three, so I'd been sleepy all day. But strangely enough, when I actually turned off the light and got into bed, I didn't feel sleepy anymore. Instead, I just felt really lonely, and I started thinking about all kinds of stuff.

I knew it. I should have given in and gone with them to Hawaii. But if I had, it would have just been the same. If only just one person in my family understood why I preferred the world of fantasy to reality. Even my dad didn't really get it.

Well, there was nothing to be done, because I couldn't really explain the "why" part myself. Grownups called feeling like this during the end of April and the beginning of the May "reality blues." It's a big time of year for everyone in Japan. It's when you're feeling down because all of a sudden everything around you changes—you move up a grade, start a new job, get promoted—and you just can't get used to it.

I wonder if that's really how it works.

If it is, then in one month you should be feeling better, after the end of May.

Was getting over this feeling I had of not knowing what to do, or where to go, whether I was asleep or awake, waiting for me in my future?

If I got careless and talked about this kind of stuff to my mom or my sisters, they'd just laugh at me and dismiss it as a stupid fourteen-year-old's view of life.

But I felt like it was all the same: being fourteen, twenty-four, or fifty-four. It's not like I ever saw one single adult around town who was full of life and vitality. They all wandered aimlessly around, looking for something stimulating, yet there was nothing in the world that could get them excited. And, well, they all looked to me as if they'd given up because they thought that's just the way life was.

I wondered, could this be the "reality blues," too?

"Ah . . ." I sighed, just to break the silence, and turned over in bed to face the window.

That's when I realized I was looking at something moving outside my window. I was on the second floor, so maybe it was a bird or something. Couldn't be, right? Birds have night blindness, so they don't fly at night. That's what I'd always heard. There might be owls in the forest, but even though the woods close by were undeveloped, this was pretty much a residential area.

A burglar? Maybe a Peeping Tom who had mistaken my window for the one in my sisters' room?

Nope, not this. It was shining faintly.

A *ghost?* I thought for a second, but then dismissed it.

There wasn't any such thing. And if there was, I wouldn't be able to see it. People who can see ghosts may not agree with me, but I think being able to see them would take some kind of special talent. So someone like me, who has no talents at all, would never be able to see a ghost.

Torturing myself like this, I figured if I couldn't sleep, maybe I could wake up and mess around with my newest figurines. I got up and glanced casually around my room. Then I saw it.

I took a breath and forgot to exhale.

She was between my study desk and my bookcase.

A girl with long hair halfway down her back. She wasn't wearing any clothes. She didn't even have on any underwear. In other words, she was naked. She was sitting on the floor, without a stitch of clothes on her, hugging her knees to her chest.

What's more, she was transparent. I could see right

through her to the other side. A faint light shone from all over her body.

Still, however you looked at it, she didn't seem to be a real live human being.

A ghost.

For sure.

I *knew* it was, and yet I didn't scream. Because the ghost was extremely pretty. I'd have been ashamed to scream at a ghost of a girl of incredible beauty, prettier than any of the girls at the junior high I went to, prettier even than a celebrity. I couldn't look away, I couldn't run away, and no way did I have the courage to talk to her, so I just sat there on my bed like a lump, my mouth hanging open in shock.

As I sat there staring, the outline of the ghost flickered as it took shape in the darkness.

From the looks of her pale body and face, she seemed to be about the same age as me. Her eyes were large, and I thought her right and left eyes looked like they were different colors. Her right eye was brown, but her left eye was kind of grayish. At least, it wasn't brown.

As I watched her in this way, it got difficult to breathe. I thought maybe it was a spell, but I'd only stopped breathing out of surprise. I laughed at myself for acting silly. I didn't think the ghost girl was looking at me with any hostility. I felt the tension leave my shoulders and my courage come back. Resolutely, I got out of bed. I'd gotten to the point where I wanted to talk to her.

Are you dead? Why are you naked? What do you want with me?

If I asked this and there was no answer, then I would know that what I was seeing was a dream or hallucination, and if it was, maybe I was feeling really depressed from stress. Tomorrow morning, as soon as I woke up,

I'd go into my mom's room, get her health insurance card out of her dresser, and go straight to the hospital.

While I was thinking this, the pale shining girl came a little closer. And then she smiled a little, and slowly stood up, covering her chest and lower body with her hands, as if she was kind of embarrassed.

I was surprised. Ghosts got embarrassed, too?

As I thought this, she appeared strangely bewitching, and my heart started to beat faster. However, in the next minute, that feeling evaporated.

Because the ghost suddenly flew right at me.

"Arrgh!" I let out a scream and fell on my butt. Then a battery that had been rolling around on the floor got crushed underneath me and let out a pop. I felt a dull pain. Then I realized that although I felt like I'd been half dreaming, there was no mistake. I was awake.

"Wh-where's the ghost?"

Quickly I looked around and turned on the light.

There was nothing there. Had it been an illusion after all? No, it had not been. I had really seen it.

Really clearly. Either that, or something had happened to my head.

I started to worry and smacked myself in the temple.

It wasn't an illusion, said a voice inside my head. A girl's voice, mixed with noise like static from an AM radio.

I knew it, I *was* going nuts. Now I was even hearing things.

I was going to the hospital first thing tomorrow.

You are not *hearing things, and you don't need to go to the hospital!* came a feminine voice.

"Huh?"

That voice again. Of a girl about the same age as me. Like one that would come from the naked ghost.

Huh? It couldn't be . . .

"Are you that ghost I just saw?"

Don't say that! I'm not a ghost. I'm as alive as anyone.

"What *is* this?! Are you inside my head? Oh, I get it. I'm possessed, aren't I! You flew right at me and then . . ."

Now that you mention it, maybe possession is what this is. But that doesn't sound very scientific, and I don't like it at all. Makes me sound like an evil spirit.

Gradually her voice became clearer. The radio static cleared. It sounded like a small person had taken up residence inside my ear.

Help me.

I panicked. I tried to hit that head of mine with someone else's voice inside it with my fist and then I yelled really loudly. But no sound came out. My fists, which were supposed to be beating on my head, hit nothing and I sat down, as if my body was being controlled by something outside of me.

Relax. I'm not a ghost. I'm a living person. I've just put some of my thoughts into your body, is all. Get it? It's mental projection. The phenomenon is called an out-of-body experience.

"Ou-out-of-body experience?"

I'd heard of it. Maybe on one of those summer special TV shows about the supernatural they're always doing. Supposedly, it was a phenomenon where somebody's soul left their body and wandered around.

Yes, that's it. I have the ability to do that.

I hadn't even said anything, but she'd read my thoughts and answered.

My body is located about a quarter of a mile from this house. That's why I sent out my soul, or rather a piece of my consciousness, from there and came to your room. Do you understand what I'm telling you?

"I kind of do, and I kind of don't . . ."

Geez! You're slow! Just believe me, 'kay? You saw me just now, right? That piece of my conscious thought. Because I tried like crazy to materialize in front of you so you could see me.

"I saw you . . . n-naked."

"Eeek! You looked?"

"You showed me. Didn't you say that just now?"

I didn't want you to see me naked. But in my case that's just how it turns out.

"It does? That's kinda inconvenient."

Inside my head she gave a little giggle.

You're funny.

Was this a compliment? Or was she making fun of me?

Either one was okay with me. It seemed like this person inside my head was pretty nice.

"Who are you? Do you have a name?" I asked boldly.

Of course I do. I'm Ayano. "Aya" is like the Aya in the word for cat's cradle, and "no" is like General Nogi. Know who General Nogi is?

"Nope."

Me neither. A long time ago my mom said I should answer like that if anyone asked me about my name. I'm fourteen.

"Th-the same as me."

What's your name?

"Kakeru. That's 'Hase' like the character for 'hasten to join' and 'se' like the character for 'sho' in 'flying.' "

You're name's Kakeru . . . Kakeru, right?

"Yeah. And?"

I just knew it! I'm sure of it! And if Jôi was right then you —

"Huh? If who was right?"

Oh, nothing. Nice to meet you, Kakeru—

"Oh, uh . . . nice to meet you, too."

I considered things while I made the proper responses. If she really had an out-of-body experience to come see me, then what for?

All I did was think it, but the answer came right back at me.

We're in a tight spot. We need help. That's why I came here to look for you.

"You came to look for me? What do you mean? And what do you mean, 'you need help'?"

It'd take too long to explain. Listen, will you come with me? I want to introduce you to the others.

When Ayano said this, there wasn't time to consent before my body stood up. Having my own body move totally against my will was kind of creepy.

"All right! But don't move my body around for me anymore."

Sorry . . . Will you come? Please, Kakeru?

Mentally I was putting together her voice, which sounded pretty grown-up for a girl of fourteen, with the form of the naked girl I'd seen. I was scared, but I felt like I'd regret it more if I turned her down flat. I was being uncharacteristically brave.

Yep. I thought I'd take a step away. From the usual.

Hadn't I decided to stay by myself for a week because I felt that something different from my old life was waiting for me?

"Okay, I'll go. So could you go out for a minute? I want to get dressed."

She laughed. *Not possible. Right now, your eyes are my eyes. And why are you so worried? You saw me naked,* she answered.

I was shocked. The sight of her semitransparent

naked body popped into my head. Knowing that she would read my mind, I put the brakes on fast. But she seemed to feel the same way, and her sense of shyness and embarrassment came through to me.

Having someone inside of yourself is kind of strange and uncomfortable.

Wondering if she would get out any time soon, I got dressed, doing my best not to look at myself below the waist. I grabbed the flashlight that we always kept on top of the shoe cupboard and went outside.

Good thing my mom and sisters weren't home. If they asked me what I was doing and I told them, they'd take me to the hospital for sure.

The girl Ayano was still inside my head. After saying again she was embarrassed that I'd seen her naked, she gave me directions to go right up ahead or to go left at the next corner. I felt kind of like a snail being directed by a parasite that had taken over its brain, but it sure beat having her move my body around for me like she did before.

The residential area around here was new, and if you left the block you would soon find yourself in fields and forests. When land in the city was expensive, businessmen like my father who worked for midsize companies came out here and bought up the new houses and moved here in a steady stream, so the land was at one time being cleared pretty rapidly.

But then the country had gone into recession, and land got cheap again, so development had stopped. Just a short walk away, empty land was divided up into undeveloped construction plots everywhere you looked.

Guided by Ayano, I went around construction plots that were overlaid like terraced rice fields, and up an unpaved road going toward a small hill. There were no streetlights. The only help I had was from the flashlight Ayano told me to bring along.

"What *are* you? What are you doing here, anyway? Where did you come from? Are you sure you're not a ghost?"

Don't ask so many things at once. I'll tell you one thing at a time if you need to know, but otherwise it's better for you not to—

"R-really?"

Incidentally, I'm not a ghost, so that's one thing you can relax about.

No way could I relax, no matter how many times she told me.

I kept asking myself if maybe she really was a ghost who'd disguised herself as a beautiful girl, and was going to kidnap me and do something terrible to me like the ghost did in that story *Botan Doro*.

But were ghosts this cute? I was sure that Oiwa in *Ghost Stories of Yotsuya* had a big lump above her eye . . . but then the ghost in *Botan Doro* was beautiful . . .

I went back and forth and back and forth in my mind, but I was curious. I was really excited to be getting away from my boring life, so I kept walking like Ayano told me to.

Walking uphill on the dirt road, which was still muddy from the rain, I spied a small wooden cabin. I had no idea why anyone would build a shack there, and the galvanized metal roof had rusted through in several places, and the outside walls were crumbling. It looked like it might collapse at any moment.

There. Go on in.

"What? Into that cabin? You sure it won't fall down?" I called out, but there was no answer. That buzzy feeling, like I had a parasite inside my head, had disappeared completely.

"Ayano? How come you're so quiet all of a sudden? Is anything wrong?"

It was no good, as I knew it would be. Now what was I going to do? Should I go into that ruin of a cabin like she told me to, or should I forget the whole thing and buy myself a midnight snack at the convenience store on my way home?

I paced back and forth in front of the cabin for about twenty seconds, and at last I resolved to do just as Ayano asked.

Yep. Wasn't I the one who was thinking that I wanted to do something different just now, like maybe see a ghost?

Really seeing something that looked like a ghost, even if she said she wasn't one, not to mention one that was totally beautiful and that had asked for help, was getting pretty close to the world of the extraordinary.

It'd be too bad to go back to my old, boring life now.

I summoned all my courage and laid my hand on the door of the old, tumbledown shack.

Creak! It actually opened with a *creak*, just like the door of a haunted house always does in the movies.

The inside was dark and had a cloying, moldy scent.

I shined my flashlight first on the ceiling, then on the walls from left to right, and then on the floor to assess the situation inside.

Suddenly the circle of light from my flashlight fell upon something lying on the floor. Could it be a person?

"What . . . is that?" I prodded it with my toe.

Suddenly a hand shot out of the darkness at my chest.

"Ah!"

I grabbed the hand, shocked.

The next thing I knew, I was blown back out of the shack by the shock of a sudden gust.

"Stop, Xiao Long!" a voice came from inside the cabin. A girl's voice. A husky voice that I'd heard before. No, maybe it'd be better to say that I'd *felt* that voice before.

There was no mistaking it. It was the voice of Ayano, the ghost girl who'd been inside my head until moments before.

"Uh . . . Ayano, are you there?"

I got up, ignoring the pain in my chest.

A short boy stood framed in the dark doorway. He was probably a year or two younger than me. A little over five feet tall and thin. Almond eyes peered out from behind long bangs.

He was wearing a torn, muddy, long-sleeved T-shirt that might have once been white, and baggy gray brocade pants. He also wore a beaded necklace that looked something like a Buddhist rosary.

With his skinny arms hanging loosely at his sides, he had the look of a lost child who'd been out in the rain crying.

Frankly, he wasn't at all what I'd expected. Had it really been this kid who had blown me back ten feet?

How on earth had he done it? Did he use martial arts or something? Now that you mention it, she *did* call him Xiao Long, or some Chinese-sounding name like that . . .

"It's all right, Xiao Long. I brought him here." A girl pushed him out of the way. It was Ayano, for sure. The naked girl holding her knees in the corner of my room whose body glowed like a ghost was really standing in front of me, a living human being.

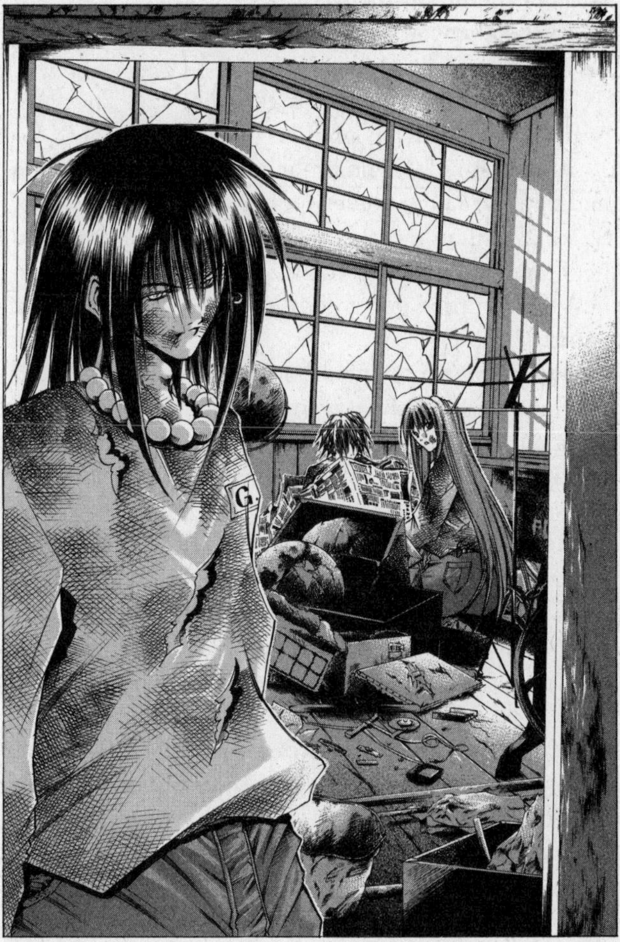
G.

This time she was wearing clothes, but they were ripped in places and looked awful.

But everything else about her was the same as when I'd "met" her in my room.

Eyes so big you could fall into them. And different colors on the right and left.

The real Ayano had pale translucent skin. The ghost Ayano hadn't been any prettier.

At this point I was finally able to believe what Ayano had said. Or rather, believing her was my only option. She had had an out-of-body experience and projected her consciousness to my room. And then her consciousness had returned to her body and she was now in front of me.

There was simply no other way to explain such an incomprehensible situation.

"I'm sorry, Kakeru. Are you hurt?" Ayano came toward me and gently stroked my cheek with a long finger.

"Oh, uh . . . no, I'm fine. I'm not hurt." I flinched, and without thinking, grabbed her hand.

It was surprisingly cold. Like the hand of a corpse. Did it have something to do with her mental projection?

Embarrassed, she took back her hand.

"I'm sorry, I got some dirt on your cheek," she said as she showed me her dirty fingertip. "Come in. The others are in here."

When I pointed at the short boy who stared at me unblinkingly, Ayano gave a slight nod.

"There's another one named Jôi. He's our leader. He's injured."

"Your leader?"

Which meant they were part of some kind of group that was doing something?

"He's terribly weak. If we don't get him to a warm place to rest up, he will die. Please, Kakeru, help us."

Weak? Die?

The back of my neck prickled. I had a bad feeling about this. Had I gotten myself into something bigger than I could ever have imagined?

As it turned out, I had.

CHAPTER 2

THE FUGITIVES

They'd put Jôi to bed in the middle of the tiny cabin.

He was wrapped in lots of newspaper, just like a glass bowl packed up with care.

I could tell, even by flashlight, that he was incredibly weak. His long wet hair was plastered to his forehead, and he had no color in his cheeks. His mouth was half open, and he didn't seem to be breathing. His eyes were squeezed so tightly shut it looked like they'd never open again.

"H-he looks dead." The words slipped out under my breath before I could stop them. I shut my mouth firmly.

However, Ayano and Xiao Long didn't get upset. They just sighed, and I could see from their faces that they agreed with me.

"The truth is, if I hadn't been treating him, he would have died already," said Xiao Long, with just a trace of an accent.

"Treating him? You mean, *you're* a doctor, Xiao Long?" I asked, and then hurriedly denied it. "Oh, no, how could you be? You look like a sixth or seventh grader."

"He has the power to heal people and animals. Do you know what *qigong* is?"

"Um, let's see, it's that thing where you hold your palm out like this and breathe deeply, isn't it? You can knock people down from a long ways away. Hey, that impact that threw me out of here just now, was it . . . ?"

"That was definitely *qigong*, but really it's something you use to heal illness and stuff. Xiao Long can use chi to heal people. It's like a miracle. But when it comes to serious injuries like this, it looks like it's beyond even his help. Even so, stuff like broken bones or damage to internal organs or blood vessels heals hundreds of millions of times faster than usual."

"Wow! Really?"

A miracle like that would make even Jesus Christ turn green with envy.

"It's true, Kakeru. Jôi broke three ribs when he was dashed against the riverbank. He hit his head hard, too. He has serious internal injuries. His lower body is black from internal bleeding." Xiao Long calmly reeled off the list of injuries like he was reading them off the medical file of a car crash victim.

"With all that, it's amazing he's still alive."

"But now his bones have set, and the internal bleeding has stopped, but he hasn't regained consciousness."

"Why?"

"I don't know. Perhaps my treatment came too late."

"That's not true, Xiao Long!" Ayano lost her temper.

"Jôi said everyone would survive. That's why all of us jumped off the cliff into the river, right? And you and I survived, just like he said we would. I'm sure Kaito's alive somewhere as well. So why would it be too late for Jôi?" Ayano's voice broke off, and she wiped her eyes.

"You have that much faith in him?"

I mean, jumping off a cliff into a river just because someone told you that you wouldn't die was absurd behavior.

"It's not like that. Jôi knows things. Jôi's the one who told us about you," answered Ayano.

"What do you mean?"

"You had better stop, Ayano."

"Xiao Long . . ."

"That's the one thing we shouldn't tell someone who's not one of us. Kakeru, it is better you not hear. It's for your own good."

At his words, something inside me snapped. "What the hell do you mean? You can't just bring me to a place like this in the middle of the night and not tell me what's going on! What do you want me to do? If you're going to behave like this, I'm going home!"

Ayano stopped me as I tried to stand up.

"Kakeru, wait. I'm sorry. I didn't mean it like that. Neither did Xiao Long."

"Well then what *did* you mean? And tell me what's going on. I haven't heard anything yet. I have no idea what's going on here. Start at the beginning. Who are you and where are you from? Why do you have strange powers? How did the three of you get so beat up?"

"I'll tell you," said Ayano. "We ran away. From this place called the Greenhouse. Me, Xiao Long, Jôi, and Kaito—another one of us who isn't here with us right now. . . ."

"The Greenhouse? What's that?"

"It's—" Ayano started to speak but Xiao Long said "Ayano!" in a low voice, stopping her.

"What is it, Xiao Long?"

"There's someone out there. Near the shack. I feel their chi."

"What? Y-you don't mean the Farmers have al- read—" Ayano said.

"Farmers? Uh, you mean like . . . the people who grow crops and stuff?" asked Kakeru.

"It's what the people in this organization call them- selves. They're the people who cultivate us," Ayano replied.

"*Cultivate* you?" This got more and more confusing. The more I listened, the less I understood.

But it seemed like a sure bet that there were some people around this old shack.

Suddenly I was scared. Sure, I had wanted some- thing out of the ordinary, but I'd never wanted to get wrapped up in anything like this.

"Now that I think about it, I'm going home. I can see you're in a tight spot, but it doesn't have anything to do with me and—"

"It has a lot to do with you," said Ayano. "Sorry to say this, but you are already involved. Or at least, our ene- mies probably think so."

"Stop joking around! I am not getting involved. I'm outta here!"

"You mustn't! You'll be killed!"

"Leggo!"

Ayano seized my arm. I shook her off. Just then . . . *Crack!*

The rotted door was kicked in, and a searchlight poured in.

"Agh! No, I'm not with them!"

Two men pointed these things that looked like pis- tols at me. I put my hands up, scared out of my wits.

It was no good. They were going to kill me.

I wished I'd never come here. I was not the kind of guy that should ever try to step outside of the ordinary.

Ordinary people should find a modest amount of motivation and live ordinary lives.

And here I thought that the most excitement that someone like me, a person with no outstanding qualities whatsoever, could expect, was that maybe if I lived a peaceful life, I'd live to be over a hundred and have the honor of becoming the oldest living person in Japan and getting my name and a picture of my smiling face in the newspaper.

Instead I was going to get killed right then and there and get my name in the newspaper for having died an unnatural death.

I sighed. What had my fourteen years of life come to, anyway?

Thup.

There was the sound of a dull impact.

Something grazed my upper arm and passed over my shoulder. At the same time, the sounds of bullets exploding came from behind me.

I'd been shot.

But they'd missed.

The man who'd shot at me clicked his tongue in disgust.

"Don't move, kid," he said, putting a foot inside the cabin with his gun raised. Another man stood in the doorway, moving his gun back and forth as he scanned the area.

Help. Ayano, Xiao Long. Where are you? I won't desert you and run off by myself. Please . . .

I wanted to scream, but no sound came out.

I thought of shutting my eyes tight and just giving up, but I couldn't do that, either.

Oh, I was going to die. Did it hurt to be shot with a pistol? I'd probably bleed. Would I understand what was happening? Would I see a field of flowers right before I died? Don't they call that a near-death experience? Probably a bunch of memories would just go around and around in my head, like a shadow picture lantern. And what was a shadow picture lantern, anyway? I had no idea. But still, this was definitely not good. If I died here, what was going to happen to that porno book I hid under my mattress? My mom would find it and my sisters would see it . . .

All these stupid thoughts went through my head in the space of one or two seconds. If this was the last slide of the slideshow of my life, it really wasn't all that interesting. What a worthless ending.

No, I absolutely did not want to die. I had to get away—somehow.

Then there came the moment when everything changed.

A man was coming toward me with a pistol. His arms suddenly fell loosely at his sides, and he started to sway like a drunk. Then, like a tin toy that has wound down, he jolted to a stop.

"Hey, what's up?" His buddy standing in the doorway called out when he realized something was wrong. Suddenly the first one turned abruptly and shot his friend.

"Ah! Wh-what're y—" The man who had been shot frantically tried to get his gun up in time when his buddy turned on him, but took the next blast full in the stomach. He was thrown over backward, then lay still.

The man who had shot his buddy next pointed the pistol at his own thigh, pulled the trigger, shooting himself, and fell down with a thud, like a mannequin that had been pushed over. I was dumbfounded.

"What was that? What just happened?" I yelled, frightened and shaking, running around in panic.

"That was close, Kakeru."

I didn't know where he'd hidden himself, but there was Xiao Long, patting me gently on the shoulder.

"X-Xiao Long! What was with that guy? Why did he suddenly shoot his friend?!"

"You experienced it earlier, didn't you? Mental projection."

"What?"

"Ayano possessed one of them and made him shoot the other one."

I was surprised. True, she'd taken over my body and moved me around a little bit. But being able to take over someone's body and move it around any way you want made her like an evil spirit from a horror film.

"Sh-sh-she killed them? Th-they . . . they're dead?" My mouth opened and closed like a fish. I couldn't speak.

Xiao Long patted my shoulder twice more. "Please calm down. No need to worry. That wasn't a gun. It's called a paralyzer, a kind of tranquilizer gun. It doesn't kill them."

"Where's Ayano?"

"Her body's over there." Xiao Long pointed to a corner of the cabin. Eyes closed, Ayano sat there as stiffly as a doll. With her lips slightly parted, she looked literally like a spirit's cast-off shell.

"It looks as if she hasn't regained consciousness yet. She's probably looking around outside to see what's going on."

"Who are these guys? You called them Farmers . . ."

"We escaped from a secret facility three days ago."

"Secret facility?"

"Do you really want to know?"

"Of course."

"Are you sure you won't regret it? If I tell you, there will be no going back."

"Aren't I involved already? And if I am . . ." To be honest, I was scared. But common sense was beaten out by seething curiosity.

"Tell me, Xiao Long. I'll have no regrets!"

"All right. Afterward, I will tell you everything."

"After what?"

"We don't have time for that now, Kakeru!" Ayano said as she suddenly awoke. She'd come back to her body.

"How does it look out there, Ayano?"

"Right now it looks like it was just the two of them. But as long as they're tracking us, we don't know when the Farmers are going to come again. Quickly, let's get out of here!" Ayano and Xiao Long took the stun guns from their enemies and tucked them in the belts of the pants they were wearing.

Ayano's words made me a little anxious. What exactly did she mean by "tracking"? Maybe they had some kind of detection device attached to them somewhere? If they did, then even if we managed to get away this time, our pursuers would only catch up to us later.

"Kakeru, can you carry Jôi on your back?"

"Huh? Me?"

"You're the only one there is. Xiao Long's only twelve and I'm a girl."

"Bu-but . . ." I had no confidence in my physical strength. Not to mention I didn't know how I was going to get down a muddy mountain road carrying someone who looked to be a good three inches taller than me.

"Please . . ." Ayano's large eyes looked into mine, glistening with tears.

I found myself nodding. "Uh, okay."

"Thank you!" Ayano squeezed my hand happily. I

couldn't back out now, in front of her. Grudgingly, I hefted Jôi up onto my back.

Jôi was tall for fourteen, but he was skinny and so felt fairly light.

Maybe I'd be able to carry him after all.

"Um, Kakeru, do you think you could carry Jôi to your place?" asked Ayano.

Impossible. It was too far to carry him on my back, and we'd definitely be noticed on a residential street like this one. A police officer might try to stop us.

"No, my house is not a good idea. But, oh, right . . ." Someone's face came to mind. I was sure that if we explained what was going on that "that person" would find it interesting and invite us in.

"Actually, I have a place in mind. Let's take him there."

"Really? Where is it?"

"School. There's someone there I know very well." I looked at my watch. It was just past ten o'clock. It was likely that no one else would be around at this hour.

"Come on, let's go. I can't carry him like this forever."

"That's true. Hurry . . ."

"Ayano, wait. Let's take the Seekers from those guys before we go," Xiao Long said.

"True, and should we have some money, too?"

"Yes, we need some. And we've used up all we had with us."

"I'm hungry, too." Ayano and Xiao Long rifled through the Farmers' pockets, removing their wallets and some little machine with an antenna that looked like a walkie-talkie.

Was that small machine what Xiao Long had called a Seeker? What was it for?

"Is it okay to take their wallets?"

The two of them looked at each other and burst out laughing at my remark.

"Talking like that could get you killed," Ayano said, making it sound like a question, as she picked up the Paralyzer and left the shack with Xiao Long.

"N-not funny. I have a weak heart," I said as I followed after them, muttering so the two of them couldn't hear.

The caretaker was waiting for us at the school gate, alerted by a call I had made from a public phone. Although it was the end of April and the nights were cool, the caretaker was dressed in a T-shirt and gray sweatpants that were slightly dirty.

"You've done good, Kakeru. That was hard work carrying him on your back all the way to school from where you were. I'm impressed." Akira Hiyama took Jôi from me, carrying him piggyback. I was about to fall over. "Geez, even though he's tall, this little boy's pretty light."

Although Hiyama-san spoke in a gruff and masculine way, the school's caretaker was actually a woman. I'd never asked her how old she was, but my guess was probably twenty-seven or twenty-eight.

She had a boyish haircut, wore plain and simple clothes, and had a rough-and-tumble manner. She looked just like a man except for the swelling under her T-shirt that indicated she was truly a lot of woman. Her chest was way bigger than my mom's or my sisters'.

Plus, when she was with me, she took off the dark sunglasses that she wore when dealing with teachers or other students, so I knew she was really quite pretty. Although she was definitely someone who would *thwok*

you on the head and give you a noogie if you didn't watch what you said to her.

Hiyama-san's job seemed to be both the school's handyman and night watchman. She lived in the janitor's room off to one side of the school grounds and drew a salary.

She was quite the enigma, and there were a lot of rumors about her going around among the students, like maybe she'd done something bad and was on the run, or that she was the only child of a wealthy family but hated that lifestyle and was living here in secret.

You might find it surprising that our night watchman was a woman, but she was much stronger than most men. Once, four or five ninth-grade punks had snuck into the school at night with the intent of doing something bad to her, but they'd got tossed out on their sorry butts in nothing flat.

On top of that, the punks were really humiliated when they were found early the next morning stripped naked in the school garden. That was the last time any so-called tough guy had dared lay a hand on Hiyama-san.

"I-I'm sorry to bother you so late at night . . ." I said. My knees were shaky and my arms felt so heavy they were numb.

"Humph. Don't worry about it. Just come inside. You two as well." Hiyama-san headed into the school, carrying Jôi, who was taller than she was, lightly on her back.

"Not a teacher, is she?" Ayano whispered in my ear.

"Nope. She's the school handyman and night watchman. We have the same interests, so we got to be friends."

Hiyama-san collected figurines. If you went into the

room where she lived and opened the doors of her frosted-glass cabinets, instead of dishes you'd find lines of handmade figurines that only a very unique person would choose to make. But sometimes she could be a little ham-handed, so she had asked me to come to the school staff room and fix up some of the figurines she'd made.

I don't think she did this to pay me back or anything, but once, when I was in the seventh grade, some ninth graders took my wallet, and she returned it to me almost before I knew it. None of those older students would ever make eye contact with me in the hall after that, so I bet she did something pretty bad to them.

"She's kind of unusual, but a really good person," I whispered in Ayano's ear so Hiyama-san wouldn't hear. If she heard me call her a good person, she'd *thwok* me on the forehead again. I think in actuality she was just extremely shy and had a hard time taking compliments.

Hiyama-san carried Jôi into her room inside the school and put him down on her unmade bed. She always left her futon out. Then she took his pulse.

"I see. He's really weak. Lemme get some food into him," she said, and rummaged around in the fridge, pulling out some bread and some juice. "You must be hungry, too," she said, throwing some to Ayano and Xiao Long before putting some in her own mouth.

"Hiyama-san, what are you doing? What's gonna happen if you eat that all yourself?" I said.

"Idiot," she replied, her mouth full, and then went over to her futon and covered Jôi up.

"Ahh!" a yell slipped out.

Hiyama-san had given Jôi a kiss.

"Why'd you do *that*, Hiyama-san? Don't tell me you're going to start doing that all the time. Oh, yeah, and you may think he's cute and all, but he's only four-teen. The same age as me. Is it okay to do that? People will think you have a Lolita complex . . . no, I guess if it's a guy who is a lot younger that's not what you call it, uh . . ."

I was flustered. Hiyama-san got up and whacked me on the forehead so hard I felt it ringing clear to the back of my head. "Idiot!" she said. "Why would I do a thing like that? I am giving him food this way. He needs all the food he can get, and if he doesn't get some sugar into him, he's going to get weaker and weaker! Don't you know that this is the best way to help a sick person or infant?"

"Oh, yeah. Right. Ha ha ha. Sorry!"

Ayano and Xiao Long swallowed their laughter, sounding like pigeons.

My face bright red, I said, to cover up how embarrassed I was, "And how's it working? Is he swallowing?"

"Yeah, somehow. Looks like his reflexes are working. Now, as for you two over there . . ." She turned to face Ayano and Xiao Long. "I heard about you on the phone from this fool, but, frankly, I still don't get it. Could you tell me properly from the beginning?" she said, sitting herself down in front of them Indian style.

Without emotion, they began to speak. Truthfully, it was even hard for me, who had seen their powers and been face-to-face with the Farmers who pursued them, to believe their story.

The facility they had escaped from was called the Greenhouse and was in the mountains, about six miles from this town. There were dozens of boy and girl psy-chics, or rather, people with psychic abilities, living there.

They were being held there because of their psychic

potential, and were trained to develop their abilities. Out of all of them, Ayano, Xiao Long, Jôi, and this Kaito guy, who had also escaped from the facility with them, were the most promising, with top-class powers.

"I see. Boy, if that's true, that's an amazing story." Hiyama-san stubbed out the cigarette she'd been smoking, a forbidding look on her face.

"So, Ayano, does that mean you were abducted by the Farmers and taken to the Greenhouse against your will?"

"We weren't abducted. We were deceived and taken there."

"Deceived?"

"Yes. I think there are some kids who were caught and taken there by force, but not that many. Some come from the countryside, being told they'll become famous; some have just graduated high school and think they've been offered a job . . ."

"What about their parents? They don't just keep quiet if their kids don't come back, do they?"

"No, everyone who gets trained at the Greenhouse lost both parents in an accident, or were abused by their parents and taken away and placed in a foster home."

"I see. So they collected you by preying on kids who were potential runaways, so nobody would think it strange that they were gone. That story makes me sick," Hiyama-san said, striking her fist on the floor.

"Does that mean you don't have any parents?" I interjected without thinking.

Ayano gave a bitter smile, "It's not that I don't have any, it's just that I'd rather not see them."

"Huh?"

"I was abused and put in a foster home."

"I . . . I'm sorry."

"Oh, it's okay. My parents are divorced now and live apart. I don't know where either of them are or what they are doing."

I didn't know what to say. Her life had been more heartbreaking than I could imagine. I thought about how I'm always whining because my mom made me eat curry rice with onions and my mom's and sisters' clothes were hanging in my closet, and felt ashamed.

I decided I wouldn't ask any more questions about their childhoods.

Ayano continued, "The four of us knew about our powers before we were brought to the Greenhouse and we knew how to use them. That seemed to be pretty rare. The Farmers called us Wild Types."

"Wild Types? What did that mean?" I asked.

"It meant our powers were naturally occurring. By contrast, the children with abilities that were created with medication, machines, or hypnotherapy are referred to as Cultivated," Ayano replied without emotion.

I was shocked.

They hadn't been treated like people at all. They lived like tomatoes in a white plastic greenhouse.

"Every day they made us do impossible things and called them 'experiments.' We were virtual prisoners. So we escaped. Following Jôi's lead . . ." Ayano said, and looked at Jôi.

Jôi's face was still pale, with no sign that he was awake. However, maybe because Hiyama-san had smoothed his messy bangs from his forehead, he looked somehow a little more alive.

"I see. I think I understand so far," said Hiyama-san, lighting her next cigarette. "Even so, I still have a lot of questions. Like what kind of people the Farmers are, and who on earth would put up the cash to make a facility like the Greenhouse. But I have no doubt that somehow or other someone's up to something suspicious."

"You believe our story?"

"I have no choice but to believe it. Kakeru actually saw you projecting yourself outside your body. And he says he was shot with a gun, and you even have those guns or whatever they are with you now." Hiyama-san looked at the guns Ayano and Xiao Long passed over to her.

"I'm so relieved. I didn't think we'd be able to get an adult to believe us very easily. I mean, up till now, no one's believed me, even when I talked to adults around me about my power they laughed at me."

"Well, sure, ordinarily . . ."

"But still, if I showed them what I could do, then I got treated like a monster."

"Well, naturally."

"It's okay, Hiyama-san won't treat you like a monster, because she's a really unusual person, not your usual kind of grown-up." Basically from me, that was intended as a compliment.

Your typical grown-up is not the kind of person I could talk to about things as they really were. Adults could never understand the kinds of things us kids really wanted to do, or that interested us, and they always tried to get us to do boring things that we weren't interested in.

Somehow Hiyama-san took my words in a good way. "Tch. An unusual person just like you," she said, and rudely breathed out smoke through her nostrils to hide her embarrassment.

"Please, Hiyama-san. Hide us for a while. If they catch us and take us away, I don't know what they'll do to us. Please!" Ayano clung to Hiyama-san and bowed her head many times.

"Mmm. But this is a school."

"I know it's not easy, but please, Hiyama-san. As a favor to all of us," I begged.

"Hey, hey, Kakeru. Looks like you're their friend now, but are you all right with that?"

"All right with that? What do you mean?"

"These kids have a powerful enemy. I mean, they've gathered up boys and girls with psychic abilities from all over the country. They've gotta have someone strong behind them to back them, no doubt about it. Could be an individual so rich that it defies the imagination, or even a government organization."

"The government? You mean, Japan's?"

"Nah, I don't really know. Maybe some foreign government. But there've been rumors for years that armies are developing psychic abilities to use in wars."

"Is that true?"

"Yeah. Apparently the former Soviet Union had a branch like that. In America the Pentagon's probably still doing it now."

"You know a lot about it, Hiyama-san. I wouldn't expect that."

"You wouldn't?"

"I thought you were the physical type."

"Pardon me? Did you think I was all muscles clear into my skull? My creed is that a perfect psyche must lodge in a perfect physique. I do kenpo and weight training and then in college . . . okay, enough of that. You have to figure that if you just go ahead and get involved, that this will be one nasty fricking opponent."

"Everybody! Come here!" yelled Xiao Long from his post at Jôi's pillow. "Quickly! Jôi's saying something!"

"He's awake?!" Ayano hurried over to Jôi's pillow.

"I don't know. But it seems as if he's trying to say something."

We made our breath quiet trying to hear him.

"What's he saying?"

"Shh. Kakeru, I can't hear. Let me handle this," Hiyama-san ordered us as she went close to his pillow to listen.

Jôi's bloodless lips moved faintly. It was unmistakable. He was trying to say something. Since I was not close to him, I couldn't hear very well, but I thought I heard the word *Yokohama* in there somewhere.

I gave up trying to understand what he was trying to say, and instead studied his profile: a high-bridged, narrow nose; long, slanted eyes; long lashes. He didn't seem to be only half Japanese, but with his name being kind of different, I thought he might be a quarter Western, or maybe half that. He was a handsome kid, enough so that if he opened his eyes and stood up, he'd make the girls go crazy. But he was maybe a little too perfect-looking, so the impression he gave was a little cold. While I looked at him so closely, I thought his eyelashes fluttered a tiny bit.

I stared harder.

"He's trying to open his eyes!" Ayano yelled.

"Jôi, you're awake, aren't you! It's me, Ayano! Xiao Long's here, too!"

There was no answer, but it was certain he was trying to open his eyes. Slowly his eyelids lifted. His eyes looked dull, and held no spark of thought. However, he looked at me quite directly.

And then, with a faint smile on his lips he murmured, hoarsely, "Kakeru . . ." and shut his eyes again firmly.

Xiao Long kept yelling his name.

But his eyes did not open again.

I was agitated.

We'd just seen each other for the first time today,

and never exchanged as much as a single word. How did he know my name? In addition to being surprised by this, I experienced an even more confusing sensation. I felt as if I'd met him, met Jôi, somewhere before. Not just passed by him on the street once or twice, that's not what I mean. What I'd see in his eyes was the feeling of a close friend, the nostalgia of seeing an old childhood buddy again, who had been far away. But it couldn't be. I'd never heard the name "Jôi." Even supposing he had been an old friend from when I was in kindergarten, I didn't have even a trace of a memory of him.

I was overcome with surprise.

"He called your name, didn't he?" Hiyama-san whispered in my ear.

Silently I nodded.

"Did the kid open his eyes at all before you came here?"

This time I shook my head silently.

"Which means it's gotta be ESP. What kind of powers does this Jôi have, anyway?"

Even Hiyama-san, usually so clever, was perplexed. But at the same time, I could see she was getting even more curious and excited. A feeling of indignation that a suspicious group of characters would chase a group of young kids this hard was bubbling up in her, I could tell. That's the kind of person Hiyama-san was.

"Well, it's obvious I can't just dump you brats out on the street, now, can I? I guess I have no choice. Guess you'll just have to stay here for a while. However, just this boy. I don't have enough futons for everybody."

"Oh, yes! Thank you!" Ayano ran her fingers through her hair as if to settle herself, and grabbing Xiao Long's sleeve to pull him away from watching Jôi just for a moment, they both bowed their heads low in gratitude.

"All righty then. Well, Kakeru, the other two can stay with you at your place."

"Huh? A-at my house?"

"Of course *at your house*. It's perfect. Your family's away on vacation. Didn't you tell me you were going to be by yourself for the whole week?"

"W-well yeah, but . . ."

"Well then, let them stay that long. You're friends now, right?"

Ayano and Xiao Long looked at me and smiled.

"O-okay, all right . . ." was the only answer I could give. It would be fine while my mom and sisters were away, but I had the feeling I was getting in deeper and deeper.

"Okay, it's settled. Okay, Kakeru, take Ayano and Xiao Long back home with you."

Already she was addressing them without using "san." In my case, she had dropped using "san" with my name the day I met her. I remember being happy, feeling like I had a new older brother—no, an older sister.

"Oh, just a moment, Hiyama-san."

"Yeah? What is it, Kakeru?"

"What was it that Jôi said?" I had to ask or I knew I wouldn't be able to sleep when I got home.

"I didn't really understand it. But something like 'He's in Yokohama.' And I also heard something about someone named Kaito being okay or something like that."

"Kaito! Kaito's in Yokohama! I'm sure of it!" said Ayano.

"Kaito's okay, too!" Xiao Long raised his voice excitedly. They were happy to do whatever Jôi said, even when he told them to go jump off a cliff into a river. Just like an oracle.

An oracle? Wait. Could it be that his ability was . . .

"Yo, get out of here, junior high school student!" Just as I almost figured it out, Hiyama-san *thwocked* me on the forehead again.

"Go home and get ready for tomorrow."

"Get ready?"

"Yeah. Golden Week starts tomorrow, doesn't it? You're going to go with them to Yokohama to look around, aren't you?"

"Oh, Kakeru, you are?" Xiao Long clapped his hands and jumped for joy.

"Thank you, Kakeru!" Ayano squeezed my hand. All I could do was nod.

"Come on in, both of you. No one's home." I showed Ayano and Xiao Long in, locked the door, and put on the security chain. I thought the people after them might show up, although, truthfully, a locked door wasn't going to do much good if they did.

"What a nice house. It must be nice to have family," Ayano said with real envy.

She must have parents, too, but if she'd been abused, you couldn't really call that "having a family."

Out of consideration for her, I couldn't say I stayed home because I hated the idea of traveling with my mother and sisters.

"But why are you home by yourself? Why didn't you go on the trip with them?"

Only natural that she would ask, I thought. I decided to tell a lie I'd thought up on the way home.

"Because we have school on the weekdays between the Golden Week holidays. I didn't want to take off for travel, so I stayed home by myself." The truth was that at my school, half the students took the whole week off.

"Wow, you're really serious about school, Kakeru."

"Do you go to school, Ayano?"

"I haven't been to school for over a year."

Again I'd asked something I shouldn't have, so I decided to stop prying. But Ayano didn't seem to mind much. "May I go see your room?" She ran happily up the stairs.

"Huh? W-wait a sec. You can't just go in and . . ."

There was something in there I didn't want her to see. I hurried after her, but she had already gone into my room without permission. "Hey, wait, how did you know this was my room?"

"I've been here once before. Remember?"

"Ah . . ." Now that she mentioned it, I remembered she'd been naked.

"Ah, you're thinking of . . . what you saw . . . aren't you?"

"Wh-what are you saying? No way, why would I?" Could she read minds? No, it couldn't be . . .

If so, that would be bad. I wouldn't even be able to daydream about her.

My heart was beating fast. Ayano went ahead and started opening the drawers in my desk.

"Ah! Cut it out! What are you doing?"

"Ha ha! You saw me a little while ago in a way that embarrassed me, and now I want to find something that embarrasses you!"

She found it right away. All those figurines I'd shut away in the drawers.

Maybe I shouldn't have been embarrassed, because after all, they were my hobby. But I worried she would think I was a weird and gloomy kind of guy. And as my sister had pointed out, there was Princess Sara and her sexy clothes.

"Oh, how cute!" Ayano said, and picked up Princess Sara.

"Wow! Did you make all of these?"

It was not the reaction I expected—in fact, it was the exact opposite reaction they'd gotten from my sisters.

"Well, yeah. I did it all myself, including the design."

"You did? Wow!"

Ayano was looking closely at my best work. She really meant what she said. I got into the spirit of things, too.

"That girl's one of my originals, a princess named Sara. Figurines like these are a kind of art. People tell me all the time that it's a nerdy and childish hobby, but it has its own professional society with world-famous artists like Takashi Murakami."

"Do you want to become an artist, too, Kakeru?"

"No, that's not why I make . . ." Then I faltered.

I had not thought that far ahead. I had not made them because I was thinking about my future dreams or job. But I was sure I had always been painting a form of my dreams.

Yes, my dream was to be a hero. I wanted to become a strong hero, save a girl from danger, and embark with her upon an adventure. I'd been expressing that in my figures, painting my dreams.

"This one is you, isn't it? It looks like you!" Ayano picked up the "Kakeru" figure I made in one hand, and the Princess Sara figure in the other, and began to role play with them.

"Ah, save me, Lord Kakeru! I'm being chased by villains!" she said in a feminine voice. Then, switching to a masculine voice, said, "What? That's terrible! Leave it to me!"

I laughed "Ah ha ha ha" as I got out a mage to be the bad guy and added him to the play. "You dare to go against me?! I shall curse you with my magic and tear you to pieces!"

"Oh, help me!" came Ayano's voice.

In my imagination, Princess Sara was overlaid with Ayano. I'm sure that's when I started falling in love with her.

But I had no sword. So probably I wouldn't be able to protect her. More likely she'd be protecting me, like before. I couldn't do much, but the least I could do was help them to get away safely.

When we went back down into the living room laughing and tired, Xiao Long was curled up on the couch asleep. He was sucking his thumb and in sleep looked even younger than twelve.

I pulled a blanket out of the guest room and covered Xiao Long up. Ayano suggested I take a bath.

That night, Ayano slept in my room, and I slept in my parent's room, in the double bed. I moved the porn out from under my mattress and to somewhere else, of course.

Tomorrow we would go to Yokohama to look for one more boy with psychic powers. I felt that while my mother and sisters were gone, I wanted to help them as much as I possibly could.

As I got into bed, I was suddenly overcome with fatigue and fell into a deep sleep.

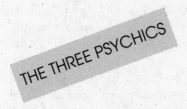

THE THREE PSYCHICS

The building looked like a paper envelope.

The white cube of a building also looked a lot like a cake box that someone had set down in the middle of the forest and then promptly forgotten about.

But despite its outward appearance, this building was known as the Greenhouse. It was called this because this strange facility, hidden away on this secluded, private lot, was licensed as an agricultural laboratory. Inside this so-called Greenhouse, however, you wouldn't find much greenery: not so much as a bunch of flowers in a vase.

The walls were white and completely bare. The floors were linoleum. Fluorescent lights in the ceiling shed cold white light in the facility's corridors twenty-four hours a day.

All day, since morning, the Greenhouse had been consumed by panic.

The Category Ones—those subjects whose powers had been cultivated to the point of actual use—had been working at combat training since after breakfast.

They were on display for the visiting members of the Frontier Committee, the founders of the Greenhouse.

Their teachers were known to the organization as Farmers. Some of these teachers were known to give their students many times the standard dose of medication, or stimulated them with electromagnetic waves of a strength that exceeded the maximum permissible level.

"Not a single one of them gets it," Arata Ikushima muttered in disgust. He was one of three senior staff members in charge of ability development at the Greenhouse.

He knew that these drugs were highly addictive and their effects often only temporary, and therefore should only be used if the subject had shown real potential. Even those with talent could be ruined forever if they became addicts and then lost the psychological strength to control their powers. The electromagnetic waves were even more dangerous: if they were administered incorrectly, they created brain tumors, sometimes resulting in the loss of valuable subjects.

Even those subjects who were successfully "cultivated" had only so much value. They could never acquire the skill and flexibility of the Wild Types, like the escapees.

The four runaways had a level of talent that put them in a completely different league altogether from Cultivated Types. They had acquired perfect command of their powers without any training at all—when they had been brought to the Greenhouse, they were already Category Ones. Jôi, in particular, was a prodigy, with a surprising gift. The secret of Jôi's power was still known only to Ikushima.

If only Jôi's power could be fully developed and tamed . . .

That was Ikushima's private ambition.

Some Farmers overestimated the usefulness of the Cultivated Types. They also thought the Wild Types could be made even more powerful with medication and electromagnetic stimulation. Ikushima militantly opposed this. He believed that Wild Types needed to learn the limits of their powers. They also had a naturally skillful command of their gifts, and so needed only the most basic training to develop.

And Ikushima had been proven right when the four Wild Types had escaped.

Ikushima never knew it was possible to have so many regrets. As he approached Director Udoh Karaki's office, he clicked his tongue in irritation.

The runaways had been in the charge of a group of new and inexperienced Farmers who had already been severely punished for their incompetence. However, Ikushima was their manager, and so also had to bear responsibility.

"Excuse me, Director." He knocked, and not waiting for an answer, opened the door. The director's office looked like a hospital room without a patient. The walls, ceiling, tables, everything, were white. Even the director's computer was white. The room was a vivid illustration of Karaki's abnormal obsession with cleanliness.

Karaki was glued to his screen. He did not even stop typing as Ikushima entered the room.

Ikushima made his footsteps loud on purpose as he approached Karaki. "It's Ikushima. Shall I apologize?"

Karaki answered without turning his head. "Did you know the Masquerade group will be arriving shortly?"

"Yes, sir, I do."

The Masquerade. That's what the Farmers called the financiers who created the Greenhouse. They came to the Greenhouse once a month—and for emergencies.

Their official name was the Frontier Committee. But since they always wore masks when they visited, the employees had started referring to them as the Masquerade.

"Ikushima, you have been summoned to this month's Masquerade, too."

Ikushima felt a cold sweat break out all over his body.

This could mean demotion. Or explusion. That is what had happened to other Farmers who had failed badly. It was said that Director Karaki had even used medication and electroshock therapy to erase their memories in order to protect the organization's secrecy, but could that really be true?

Perhaps they'd been murdered?

Even assuming they hadn't been murdered, the use of powerful medication and electroshock on cranial nerves to forcibly erase memory was bound to leave some aftereffects. And though they erased memories in small units, from a few months to one to two years, he'd heard of cases in which ten years of memory had been lost. He had earned a lot of money at the Greenhouse, but it would be of no use to him in that sort of condition; he would never lead a normal life again.

So, for the Farmers, expulsion was a fate worse than death.

Karaki saw the sweat beading on Ikushima's forehead and smiled scornfully. "No need to be afraid. Instead, consider this a chance given to you by the members of the Masquerade. They want to hear your plan. You must have some thoughts on how to capture the four that escaped. Discuss them at the meeting.

Convince the committee, and your punishment will be suspended."

"Of course, I have put together a plan. However, it will require the use of some of the Category One telepaths," said Ikushima, struggling to keep the fear out of his voice.

"Really. In that case, I'd like to hear about this plan in advance, Ikushima."

"This is an excellent opportunity to release our Category One telepaths into a real-world combat situation for the first time. And, in any case, it's our only chance to succeed. Not even skilled Farmers can catch powerful psychics like these Wild Types. So let's use a thief to catch a thief. Psychics of comparable power would be our best bet."

"Interesting. That may be a good idea. It will solve two problems at once. We might as well use this chance to try."

"Thank you."

Ikushima had not told the director everything. Out of thirty-eight Category One telepaths, no more than ten were prepared for actual combat. They were all more powerful than the four fugitives but were not yet psychologically fit for combat. Their powers were as yet newly awakened, and they hadn't yet adjusted to them emotionally. If anything went wrong, there was a real danger that they might actually kill their opponents. Jôi and the other Wild Types were rareties, and their powers were of relatively low voltage. But they had top-drawer potential, and, what was even more unusual, they were psychologically stable. If at all possible, he wanted to take them alive and bring them back to the Greenhouse for training.

However . . .

It was possible they might not have the luxury of that option.

And another failure would put Ikushima himself in a precarious position.

In the worst-case scenario, if Jôi and the others were defeated and killed by the cultivated psychics, the Masquerade would probably still be pleased with the outcome. It would be their first positive actual-combat result.

"Submit the names of the members who will be going into combat soon. So that we can present the list to the Masquerade," the director said.

"I have already gotten the best members ready and have called them here."

"What?"

"Sho, Takemaru, and Maya. I will bring them here immediately—"

"We are already here, Ikushima-san." The voice surprised him. It was coming from an unexpected direction.

Karaki also was startled. When he looked around for the voice's source, he found that a young man with dyed-brown hair had somehow entered the room and set himself down on the white sofa.

"Sho, when did you—" Even Ikushima, who knew all about Sho's ability, could not stop himself from asking the question. That was how amazing Sho's sudden appearance was. "And the other two—Takemaru and Maya?"

"Maya is waiting on the opposite side of that door, Director. May I have her show something to the both of you?"

As Sho said this, a horde of decomposing corpses appeared before Ikushima and Director Karaki—zombies.

"Arrgh!" Karaki screamed like a child. The herd of

groaning zombies descended on him like a pack of ravenous beasts.

"A-all right, Maya, enough!" shouted Ikushima, and the zombies disappeared at once.

With a faint smile, Sho next called out, "Hey, Takemaru!" in a voice loud enough to be heard outside the door. Just as he did, the chair in which Karaki sat rattled and began to dance.

"Takemaru is right outside. Shall I call him in?"

"No, no, stop it!"

Holding on to his chair so as not to be shaken off, Director Karaki said, "All right. I understand your powers quite well. It looks as if we can entrust you with this task, so listen carefully. As you may already know, your mission is to capture your fugitive comrades. You must bring them before me without fail. Take them alive if you can, but if worst comes to worst . . ."

"Hah. Leave it to the three of us. We'll take care of it." No sooner had Sho said this than he disappeared like an illusion.

After making sure they were gone, Karaki muttered distastefully, "Damn monsters."

You're the one who told us to create them, thought Ikushima. *And we're the ones who created them . . .*

The three young people who had been made into psychic monsters had already been set loose. No one knew yet what a battle to the death between psychics might be like. And not even Ikushima could imagine its awful finale.

"Kakeru, this is so delicious! And I want that big pork bun, too," said Ayano, jumping up and down like a little kid.

"Go ahead and buy it if you want. I brought all the

pocket money I have." I took out my wallet, and to the old man steaming the pork buns, I said like a cheapskate, "One, please."

Actually, on our way to Yokohama, we'd stopped to eat and drink several times, and after paying for our ticket home, I didn't have that much money left.

It had been about a year since I'd last visited Yokohama. Before my dad was transferred to Kyushu for work, he used to like to take drives on his days off, and he brought me here. My dad especially liked Chinatown, where we were, and was proud that he knew all of its intricate alleys.

But there was one place where even my dad, who loved Chinatown so much, would never set foot. It was a squalid, undeveloped area stuck to one side of Chinatown. For some reason my dad said it was not part of Chinatown. It was called the Nationless Quarter, after the shiftless people who lived there. In this dangerous area the signs were not only in Chinese, but in all the languages of the world. The atmosphere was seedy. Almost all the buildings were old and empty, and when there was an open shop, it usually sold illegal goods completely unlike what was advertised on its sign. A plan had been developed to tear down everything in the not-so-distant future, and my dad said that the place had become still more dangerous in the past few years, maybe because of the plan.

According to information Xiao Long had obtained by asking in Chinese, their friend who had escaped from the Greenhouse with them was in the Nationless Quarter. I nearly freaked out when I heard that we'd be going to a danger zone that my dad always warned me to steer clear of. So I was being extravagant, treating Xiao Long and Ayano to all sorts of stuff. Anyway, all the pocket money that I'd worked so hard to save might just get stolen. Might as well put it to use feeding ourselves well.

And seeing Ayano happy made me happy, too.

"It's delicious, Kakeru. Try some," Ayano said, breaking the steaming deluxe pork bun in half to give part to me.

I gulped down a chunk of the steaming pork bun, and the heat brought tears to my eyes.

Somehow, I was having a really great time.

Some young guys passing by turned around to look at Ayano, who was as cute and slender as a model or teen idol. Ayano was wearing a baggy T-shirt and jeans that were too big that she had borrowed from Hiyama-san, but when a girl had such a lovely face and a natural sense of style, anything looked good on her. In fact, she looked smart, stylish, and cute. I wondered how we appeared to other people. A girl who looked like a model and an average junior high school student, if I do say so myself. And a boy asking the shop owners for directions in Chinese.

Incidentally, Xiao Long was wearing some old clothes I'd outgrown that fit him perfectly. Still, Xiao Long looked cool. Of course, when I had worn them they'd been pretty average. But Xiao Long had an indefinable stylishness that should have been beyond a mere twelve-year-old.

A twelve-year-old who looked good in cast-off clothes. Yikes. *What kind of life had he lived?* I wondered as I watched Xiao Long out of the corner of my eye.

Then our eyes met. "Xiao Long, want something to eat?" I said, breaking the half of the pork bun that Ayano had given me in half again and handing it to him.

"Thank you, Kakeru. Ooh, it's warm."

Yesterday when I'd met him I thought he was expressionless, but he'd opened up while we were together and now he smiled much more often. As for me, I also felt much closer to the two of them than you might expect, considering we'd met only yesterday. We were comrades who had fought against a dangerous, gun-wielding enemy.

Although I must admit that I didn't actually do much.

Truthfully, I was thinking that it was maybe about time for me to ask what Jôi's power was, but if they got cold and distant again, I'd feel pretty sad.

Well, I was sure I'd figure it out anyway once Jôi regained consciousness. He may not have woken up yet, but Hiyama-san, who seemed to have some medical knowledge, was doing everything she could to help him recover faster.

In the meantime, the three of us had come to Yokohama to look for one of their friends who had escaped with them, a boy named Kaito who was my age.

"Kakeru, Ayano, once we cross this road, we'll be in the Nationless Quarter," Xiao Long mumbled as he stuffed the rest of the pork bun in his mouth.

"Kaito is over there somewhere, isn't he?" said Ayano.

Certainly the ambience of the stores and houses changed abruptly on the other side of the street. And not just the signs on the stores, but the people on the streets seemed somehow "nationless," too.

"I dunno, you think it's going to be okay with just the three of us walking around over there?" Suddenly I felt timid.

"You'll be fine. Xiao Long and I are with you, aren't we."

Right.

They had psychic powers.

It hadn't taken them very long to fight off an enemy armed with guns. The two of them were pretty amazing.

Thinking of it that way, I hadn't needed to work so hard to spend my money. They could flatten any punk who tried to steal it from me.

"Hurry up, you two. You'll be left behind . . ."

Ayano was impatient. She galloped across the street and headed toward the Nationless Quarter.

Xiao Long and I hurriedly chased after her.

Just by crossing the street, we were in what felt like a completely different city.

Just like my dad said, the signs were not only in Chinese, but in something that looked like English, Korean Hangul, and some that I didn't recognize at all with writing from Southeast Asia or maybe even the Middle East. There was a fair amount of pedestrian traffic, but over half of them were foreigners from Asia or the Near and Middle East. Besides, the farther we went, the more shifty old men muttering to themselves and gloomy-looking people with bleached-blond or dyed-red hair there were. Garbage lay strewn all over the streets, staining the asphalt. Trash moldered in reeking piles under all the slanting power line poles. A closer look revealed dead rats and cats as well.

"Ugh, I didn't know there were places like this anywhere in Japan," I said without thinking. Xiao Long chuckled.

"Fujian Province, where I lived until three years ago, had plenty of places that were scarier than this."

"Huh? You were in China until three years ago, Xiao Long?"

"Yes. My parents brought me to Japan. My mom was

Japanese, so I was able to get Japanese citizenship quickly and start going to elementary school, but my dad couldn't get naturalized or find a job. And two years ago, he left my mom and me here and returned to China."

"Huh? What about your mother? She must be very worried since you disappeared . . ."

"My mom left me with the old chiropractor guy who'd taken care of us, and disappeared somewhere. I could use *qigong*, so I figured I could survive by helping him with treatments."

"Oh really . . ." was all I could say.

Xiao Long smiled and spoke in such a matter-of-fact way that somehow I couldn't summon up words to sympathize. He didn't sound to me like he was after sympathy. He was proud he'd managed to support himself, I was sure. He had that kind of smile on his face.

We'd walked at a quick pace while we talked, and had come out at a dim back street where not so many people passed by. There was more graffiti on the walls, and the buildings were crumbling. Vagrants and boys in dirty clothes sitting on the bare ground stared up at us as we passed quickly by.

"Um, uh, Ayano, Xiao Long? Are you sure this is okay? We're pretty deep in, and it might be dangerous," I said.

Even Ayano spoke uncertainly, without much force. "I know, but there's nothing we can do about it. We heard that until about six months ago, a boy like Kaito always hung around with his friends in the plaza behind a building in the Nationless Quarter. That's the building over there . . ." She pointed at an old building of about ten stories that stood out. "That reminds me, Kaito said he lived with some friends close to Yokohama Chinatown for a long time. I'm sure when he got separated from us he just went back to where he was from, where his friends were."

"Think so, huh?"

Ayano suddenly looked uneasy. "What do you mean, 'think so, huh?' " she said.

"Oh, nothing. Let's go. It really is kind of scary here. Let's hurry up and find Kaito and go."

"Well, well, how unusual" came a voice mixed with contemptuous laughter.

Five guys suddenly erupted from different alleys and flew toward where we'd stopped.

"Whatcha doin' here, kiddies?"

"Scary scary?"

"Did ya come to give us money? Heh heh heh."

"Wow. There's a girl with them, Kaneko!" He used the Japanese version of a Korean surname.

"And she's really cute." Grinning nastily, the five sized us up.

Here we go, I muttered in my mind. I knew this would happen.

"Hey, I told you so, you two, *now* what're we gonna do? I'm not proud of this, but I've never been in a fight before!"

Kind of pathetic, but under the circumstances I thought I'd better come clean. I'd have to leave things to the two of them. This contradicted what I had been thinking as I fell asleep the night before. I mean, the two of them were people with psychic powers who had escaped from some creepy facility where they'd undergone special training, and I was just an ordinary junior high school student.

"All right. We'll protect you. Get behind us, Kakeru," said Ayano.

"Yes, do that please. Let us do the rest." Calmly, the two of them stepped toward the young punks.

"Well, well, what are a couple of cute kids like you going to do to us? Heh heh heh." A guy with a shaved head who had piercings everywhere on his face except his ears seemed to be the leader. He licked his lips as he approached us.

It was my first time seeing such a scary-looking guy this close up. I was shaking so hard I thought I might pee in my pants when I said, "Okay, okay, stop it, you guys. I knew it would be impossible. We should just get the hell out of . . ." and I put my hand on Ayano's shoulder.

Just then Ayano went limp, and, with a jerk, she collapsed against me. Startled, I supported her limp body, and knew that whatever I'd seen last night had begun again.

Mental projection!

At the same time, the smile on the face of the guy with the piercings disappeared unnaturally.

Ayano had possessed him!

His eyes moved up and down, right and left as if swimming in space. Slowly they turned the opposite way from us, to where his buddies stood.

"Is something wrong, Kaneko?" called a guy with long hair dyed bright red and tied back in a ponytail. The next second, the guy with piercings called Kaneko howled like a beast and went nuts.

Two of them were thrown, smacked by thick arms covered in hair flailing around at random. One was thrown through a shop window, shattering the glass with a resounding crash.

"What the hell are you doing, Dude! What're you on?" One of the punks who had slipped through Kaneko's attack reached out toward Xiao Long's chest.

But Xiao Long reached out his hand in a leisurely motion that looked like something you see old men do when they practice tai chi in the park, and put his palm on the guy's chest.

All it took was this. The guy made a strange noise like "Hao?!" and went flying. He struck the asphalt and lay still, as if someone had taken out his batteries.

This was Xiao Long using chi.

Then there was a sudden shock, like the sudden gust that had sent me flying yesterday. It was scary that he could defeat an opponent a head taller than he was with just a touch.

Kaneko was already down, having hit his own head against the wall. Only one more was left. He was sitting on his behind, not knowing what had happened, his mouth hanging open in shock.

"We don't want to have to deal with him calling any of their friends. Better put him to sleep," Xiao Long said. Narrowing his eyes coldly, Xiao Long placed his palm toward the last of the punks from a distance of six feet away.

"Gohhhh . . ." Xiao Long made a whooshing sound with his voice, doing a deep exhale from the chest. Suddenly, without warning, stacks of magazines piled carelessly in the entrances of old buildings, cardboard in the road, and plastic bags from convenience stores burst into flame.

"Aarrgh! What is this? The garbage all just caught, just caught on *fire*!" I thought I would've been used to this kind of stuff after last night, but even so, I yelled in surprise.

"It's okay. It's one of us."

Ayano had returned from her out-of-body experience. She didn't look at all surprised. She squeezed my hand reassuringly.

"He creates flames like that just by concentrating."

Is that what you called pyrokinetics? Did that mean that the other guy with psychic powers we'd been looking for was close by?

"You can stop now, Xiao Long," a voice came from the alley.

The voice was hoarse and cracked, but not entirely without a childlike quality. I'd experienced it, too. It was a boy whose voice had just changed, in other words probably about my age.

Xiao Long's almond eyes widened at the sound. "Kaito!"

Kaito appeared out of the alley slouching, with his hands in the pockets of his skinny black jeans.

"They're friends of mine. That's all you need to do for now. I'll deal with them later."

"You're alive! I knew it!" Xiao Long yelled as he ran over to him.

Kaito was tall. He stooped over and scooped Xiao Long up just like a pet dog.

"Ha ha ha ha. Sorry 'bout that, Xiao Long. You, too, Ayano," he said, making it sound like a question.

"I know. I would've gone home first thing, too, if I'd had a home to go to," Ayano said, letting go of my hand.

"Who's the little boy?" he said, pointing with his chin.

I was irritated. I wasn't a little boy.

I wanted to answer him back, but he was two inches taller than Jôi . In other words, six inches taller than me.

I dislike people who are taller than me. When I am in front of people like that, suddenly I can't say what I want to. It's probably from the trauma of all my friends who were shorter than me passing me up in height one after the other in elementary school, leaving me the shortest one in class.

I still get an unpleasant feeling just thinking about

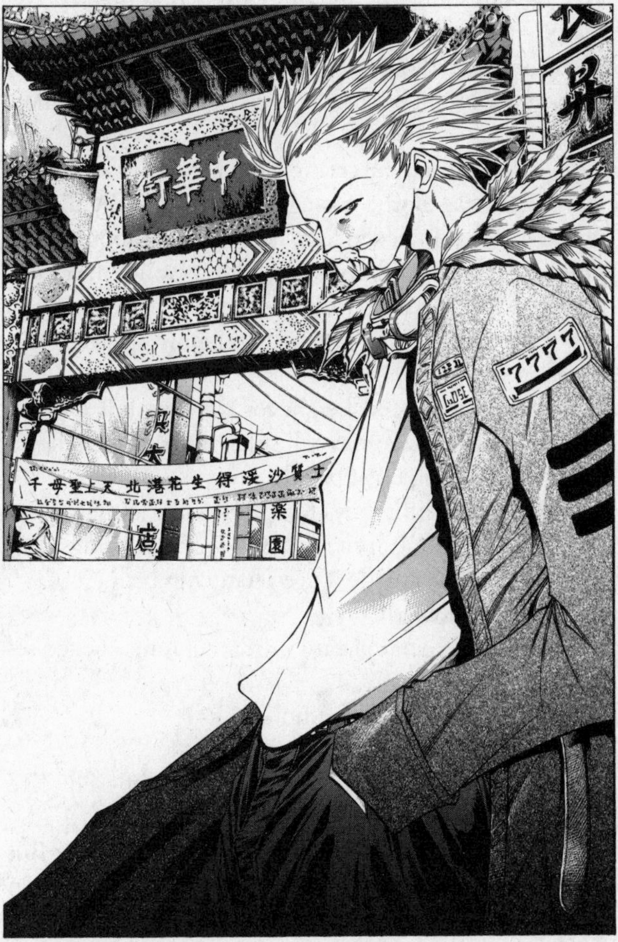
中華街
7777

that time. In elementary school, your social position in class was decided by how tall you were, which was decided by your birth month, and how fast you grew. When you suddenly sprouted up more than a few inches, at least for boys, that decided your rank in class. After they passed me in height, the classmates I used to bully started bullying me. I got in trouble for the littlest things.

This subtle vertical relationship between me and my classmates was always changing, but the bullying was not so bad that I needed to make a big deal about it. Besides, if I talked to adults about it, they would never understand. All I could do was reach an understanding within myself and try to get tall and grow up as fast as I could.

Now I was a good height for my age, but I had a hunch my self-image was still stuck in that time when I was short, looking up at people.

"He's not a little boy, Kaito. He's the same age as you," Ayano said, as if she could sense my feelings. But her consideration made it even harder to bear.

"And he's Kakeru."

"What?" When he heard my name, Kaito looked serious.

"I see. The one Jôi mentioned?"

"Um hm."

"You mean our future depends on a little boy like that?"

Their future? Me? Wonder what *that* meant. But now that I thought about it, Ayano did say she'd known me . . .

Kaito glared at me, frankly hostile.

Oh, great. It looked like I was in another fine mess. I'd only met Ayano and Xiao Long yesterday. I was as close to being an outsider as you could get. Why did they ask me to do stuff and then get mad at me?

While this was going through my mind, I gave a self-deprecating smile and said, "Nice to meet you."

Kaito did not reply and spit on the ground. "Looks like Jôi's lost his touch."

"Kaito!" said Ayano.

"I don't think you need to talk like that, either, Kaito," Xiao Long broke in. "It was because of Jôi that we escaped from the Greenhouse."

"What happened to him, Xiao Long?"

"He's all right. But he hasn't woken up yet."

"Oh yeah? He's all right?" Kaito turned his back on us. "Then go home. You shouldn't be here. You should be by your precious Jôi's side."

"Kaito!"

"You're going to forget about us and hide yourself here, Kaito?" asked Ayano.

Kaito looked at them over his shoulder, stopped them from running up to him with a look, and said, "Hide myself here? This is my town. What's wrong with coming home?"

"I don't think anything's wrong with it. But aren't we all in this together? We're friends!"

"These guys are my friends." Kaito looked at the guys Ayano and Xiao Long had defeated. Helping one another up, they gathered around Kaito and glared at us. "These kids live on the street like I do. Until I went to the Greenhouse, I'd always lived with them. While I was gone, these guys were prey for other groups and yakuza hoodlums around here, and told they'd have to work for them. But that's not going to happen with me back here. I want to protect them. So . . ." Kaito insisted, with his back to Xiao Long and Ayano. "Go home."

The two of them had nothing to say to this and hung their heads.

"You *idiots!*" yelled Kaito at the group that had attacked us, slapping their faces. "How many times do I have to tell you not to pick fights with people who aren't from around here, or shake them down! That's not going to happen anymore now that I'm back. Understand?!"

The punks, including the older ones, cowered like small dogs at Kaito's words. All of them, including the guy who had broken the glass, and the one with the piercings who had banged his head against the wall and was bleeding, listened to what Kaito said, approached us, and reluctantly bowed their heads in apology. He seemed to be the boss of the juvenile delinquents around here. And if the pyrokinetic ability I'd seen earlier was what his power was, then being the leader of a group of punks like this was a piece of cake. Nevertheless, it didn't seem like they followed Kaito out of fear of reprisal. Rather than fear from the dropouts surrounding Kaito, we felt affection.

"We're sorry. We didn't know you were Kaito's friends."

"We were wrong. For real. But wow, Kaito's power is really something. 'Course, we haven't seen it for a long time."

"If Kaito stays with us, I betcha we'll be strong again."

" 'Course we will, fool! The yakuza's not gonna shake us down for money, either. Right, Kaito?"

The guys followed after him as he left, unanimous in their praise. They really loved him. And if they did . . .

After we watched Kaito disappear down the alley with his comrades, I said to Ayano and Xiao Long, "What do you want to do? He's got friends here, and I'm pretty sure he won't come back with us."

"No, you can't!" Ayano raised her voice.

"If we lose even one of us, the Farmers will catch us for sure! Kaito's a Psycho Burner! He doesn't have to be that close to attack with flame. When he was with us, it was hard for them to get close to us. The reason we could escape is because there were four of us. If he doesn't come back to us then we'll be captured . . . killed . . . I *know* it."

"It's all right, Ayano," said Xiao Long. He comforted the shaking Ayano and said, "It's not like Kaito's going to be safe if he stays here. The Farmers probably already know he's here. And Kaito's not going to leave us in the lurch. It's okay, he'll come with us, I'm sure of it. Let's talk with him again."

Ayano nodded and stood up. "I'm sorry, Kakeru. I have a feeling Kaito gets more stubborn when you're around. That's the kind of guy he is. We do what Jôi says without question, but not Kaito."

"We'll go and talk to him again, just the two of us. So could you go home before we do, Kakeru?"

"I could do that." I'd been going to say that staying here by myself was scary, but stopped. It was broad daylight, and that group of punks had probably been drawn to us because Ayano was so beautiful. If anyone picked a fight with me, the most they'd get would be the rest of my spending money. But I would feel pretty weird going home by myself.

"Okay, I'll go back to Chinatown first and wait at that shop that sells pork buns where we went a little bit ago," I said and, leaving Ayano and Xiao Long, retraced my steps down the street at a trot.

Just when I had almost gotten out of the Nationless Quarter, it happened.

I felt faintly dizzy and stopped.

My head suddenly got heavy and my ears started to ring a little.

"Must've caught a cold."

It was possible. It had been cold last night when I'd gotten all sweaty carrying Jôi on my back.

"I shoulda told them I'd go home before them, after all."

Having said that, since neither Ayano nor Xiao Long had a mobile phone, it wasn't like I could contact them now.

"Well, whatever. I guess I'll wait at the shop where they sell pork buns and have some nice warm tea. I have enough money left for that," I said to myself as I turned the corner.

"Huh?"

Suddenly I felt uneasy and stopped.

There was nobody there. Not a single passerby or a single customer at a restaurant or bar to be seen. Around this corner it was only one more street until the entrance to Chinatown. This place should have been bustling with people. Why wasn't it?

"This is weird . . ."

I turned to look down the street I'd just come from.

"Huh?"

Nobody there, either. What was up with that?

This can't be. There were tons of people there until a second ago. Too many people to have gone away so suddenly.

What on earth was going on?

I felt my heartbeat speed up. Something was happening. And it had something to do with the walk on the wild side that I'd taken for the first time yesterday, I was sure of it.

Which meant . . . psychic powers? If so, whose? More important, what kind of power was it? It couldn't be the kind of power that made people disappear. Even psychic powers wouldn't be able to do that.

"Hey, you over there?"

A proud and sickly sweet voice came from behind me.

When I turned around, a girl was sitting by the roadside, licking a popsicle.

Thinking about it later, I realized right then that the curtain had risen. It had risen on a psychic whose power was beyond anything I could have imagined.

CHAPTER 4

PSYCHIC PATROL

The girl who had called out to me bit off the last of her popsicle, tossed the stick aside, and stood up. "You! Hey, you! What are you looking at me like that for?"

She was about the same age as me, or maybe a little older. She had the face of a cute little doll. The way she smiled at me was mysterious. And she was dressed in black from head to toe, in a black long-sleeved T-shirt and a tight black miniskirt. Even her hair was long and black. This style suited her dainty features.

What a relief. At least I wasn't alone anymore. And if so, then these strange goings-on were nothing to worry about.

"Can you see anyone?" the girl asked, persisting.

She had a cute smile, but this was no time to be thinking about such things.

Her question made me suspicious. Was she maybe the same as Ayano and the others? I intended to figure it out. "Who are you? What do you want?" I asked.

Not answering my question, she said, "If you can't see anyone, want me to show them to you?"

"Huh? What do you mean by that?"

"I mean *this*."

I thought I heard something go *thump*.

But it sure wasn't something that I heard with my ears. It was more vague than that, more like a sensation of something hitting something else. It was like a shock wave. It spread inside my head like ripples on the water.

In the next instant, something that couldn't be possible was right before my eyes. In front of me I saw myself. I appeared from out of nowhere, just as if someone had flipped a switch.

Then the me standing in front of me began to break up like an afterimage. In the twinkling of an eye suddenly I was popping up everywhere. Me, me, me, me! And all the mes looked at me at once and smiled wickedly.

Fear welled up from deep inside my heart.

"*Uwaaaaaa!*" I shouted at the top of my lungs.

If I'd had a gun I would not have hesitated to shoot myself in the head. And if I had felt this terror just a little longer, I might have fallen into a dark place and never come back again.

But that didn't happen.

All of the Kakerus that had appeared out of thin air evaporated, disappearing too quickly to leave an afterimage. I almost fell over from the shock.

Again, the place was a ghost town. A town where there was only me and the girl who would not stop smiling.

So it seemed that everything I was seeing was an illusion. No, I was sure it wasn't just that.

I had a strong feeling about this. What I was seeing right now was a lie. The truth was that until just a second ago this had been a busy downtown street. That it appeared as if there was nobody on the street besides the

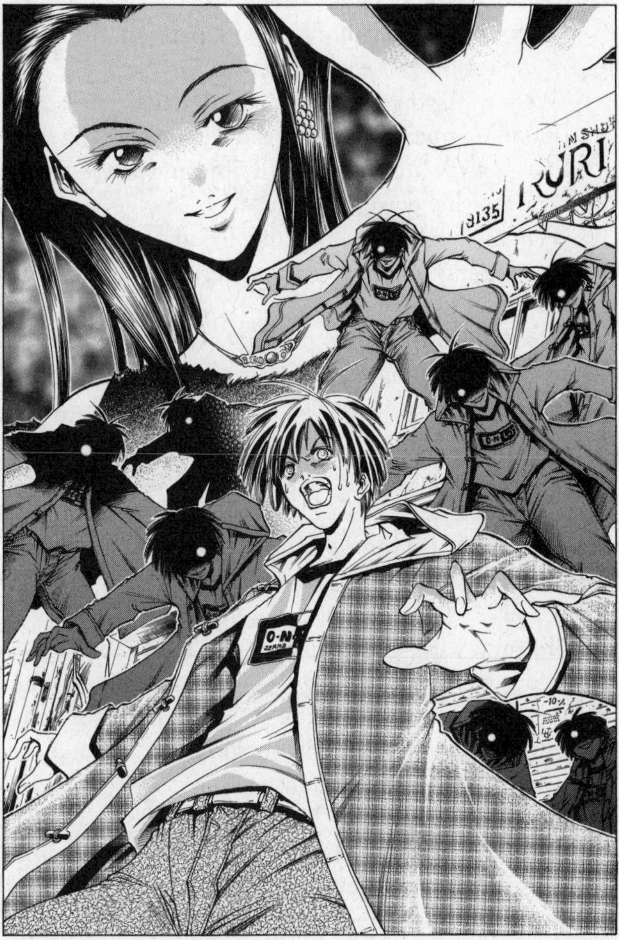
RURI
8135

two of us had to be an illusion being shown to me by the girl in front of me. It might be precisely because I was enveloped in an illusion that I was able to think so clearly at that moment.

When the girl saw that I was not particularly frightened, she regarded me with interest.

"Well, well, you don't seem afraid. Cool!"

I stood up quickly and got ready to attack.

She giggled. "You are right. This is my power."

"Power, what power?"

"Can't you tell? It's a kind of telepathy."

"Is telepathy when you can communicate what you want without speaking?"

"Yes. That's telepathy, all right. Of course, mine's stronger. I can put an image or sound directly inside a person's head, like I just did with you. Amazing, isn't it?" She giggled again.

Amazing was putting it lightly. Two or three screws had almost come loose inside my head.

"And? What's your power?" she asked, laughing gaily.

"Huh?"

"Tell me what kind of power you have! You're psychic, too, aren't you? I mean, you're hanging out with Ayano and Xiao Long, aren't you? I saw you with them. My curiosity got the better of me, so I forgot about them for now and came after you instead!"

"I-I'm . . ."

It looked like she thought I had psychic powers like Ayano and Xiao Long. What a laugh. I was a normal person. Just a completely average ninth grader.

"C'mon, c'mon, hurry up and tell me! If you don't, I'm gonna show you something scarier." She giggled some more.

What was I gonna do? I was in a bind. I should've

stayed with Ayano and Xiao Long. I mean, being seen with Ayano and the others had gotten me into this mess. That had been a mistake from the first. No, it wouldn't do any good to think that way now. Circumstances had moved too far along. I was in, and in deep.

Anyway, I had to do something, and do it quick.

When she'd showed me those countless other mes a little bit ago, I almost lost my mind, and if she showed me stuff that was even scarier, there was no way I could stay sane.

If I could somehow stall for time, Ayano and the others might show up.

"Oh, man! You're so annoying. Well? Are you going to do it or not?" She stopped smiling and looked irritated.

"W-wait a sec. Uh, what's your name?"

"My name? It's Maya. Why?"

"M-Maya? What characters do you write it with?"

" 'Ma' is the *ma* like 'hemp' in 'hemp rope,' and for 'ya,' first you write the character for 'ear' . . ."

"Oh, I get it! *That* Maya. I get it."

"And?"

"And, uh, it's a really nice name."

"You're so annoying! Shall I destroy your mind for you?"

Maya quit smiling and her eyes rolled back in her head.

Oh no! Operation: Stall for Time had failed!

"Wait a sec. Wait, Maya. How do you know Ayano?"

"Uh? Whaddya mean 'how do I know her'?"

"C'mon, just tell me!"

"Okay, it's like we're in the same class. But I hate her. You haven't asked about the Greenhouse. Oops! I said it! Sorry."

"Why say sorry?"

"We're not allowed to mention the Greenhouse. Oops, it just slipped out. Ha ha ha ha!"

"Oh, it's okay, I'll pretend I didn't hear it."

"You will? But it's no use. Now that you've heard 'Greenhouse,' I have to take you there and get your memories erased. If I can't, then . . ."

"If you can't, then what?"

"Then I'll have to kill you."

Both sides of her mouth turned up in a somewhat psychotic smile.

This was bad.

"Wait!" I gathered all the courage I could muster, and making the fiercest face I could, spread my hands wide and thrust them out. Startled by my actions, Maya stopped what she was doing.

"You *did* say you wanted to know what my ability was, didn't you?"

Imitating Maya, I pulled up both corners of my mouth. All bluff and cold sweat.

But it seemed to have an effect. Maya's smile froze.

"You've got a lot of nerve, coming after me, not knowing what my power is, Maya."

I had fired off another bluff! Maya seemed frightened. She shrank back two or three steps. Then I fired off bluff number three. "I'm warning you, Ayano and Xiao Long are under my protection."

"Those two? Protect? Whoa! Are you that powerful?" Maya froze.

All right, I'd throw caution to the wind. If I could just keep this up . . .

"I'll do you a favor, Maya. If you clear out right now, I'll forget about today. Or else you will suffer tremendously." My heart pounded as I let volley number four fly.

Maya gazed at me without speaking. I knew she was weighing the choices in her mind. Would it be better to fight this guy, whose power she didn't know, now, or should she pull back and reassess the situation?

Choice number two: it was obvious. Resetting her boundaries was obviously the best choice here! Right? Pick choice number two!

"Isn't this fun," said Maya, turning up the corners of her mouth again. "You almost never get a chance like this, to meet someone so powerful who didn't come out of the Greenhouse."

"Huh? Oh, well, really I'm not—"

"Let's give it a try. After all, I'm a Category One, too."

"Ca-Cata-Category?"

"Let's get to it, Wild Type. We're both psychics, so no need to hold back. Let's take this to the bitter end!"

As Maya said that, a sound of something bursting exploded inside my head.

Quickly I closed my eyes. I thought I'd see something terrifying if I didn't. Whether it was an illusion or something else, if I closed my eyes, maybe I wouldn't see it.

I was right. For now, I had suppressed the illusion Maya was trying to show me just by closing my eyes, and it didn't swoop down and get me.

However, just because I couldn't see it didn't mean it wasn't there.

I may have had my eyes closed, but the illusion circled around and around me, howling. It got close to my ears, and made a sound like it was going to take my head off. Then, just when I thought it had gone a little bit away from me, it came at me with a roar.

Desperately I kept persuading myself. *Don't open*

your eyes. It's an illusion. There's nothing to be afraid of as long as you don't look at it.

Don't be deceived!

"Hm. Looks like you're using your brain, Wild Type. But do you have to close your eyes like that to use your power?" Maya said, and slapped me upside the face.

I took the blow.

Whatever she did, we were still in the middle of a crowded street, and lots of people must be around.

She'd never be able to kill me here.

"Say something, you coward!"

This time she hit me with her fist. It hurt, too, even if she punched like a girl. The taste of blood spread from a cut inside my mouth.

It's okay. Endure it. If she does anything more than this someone passing by will stop her for sure. We're on a busy street corner . . .

"I'm warning you, Wild Type. No one's going to save you."

What did that mean?

"Because I'm using my telepathy to make it so they can't see you."

Huh?

"So right now you're the invisible man, sweetie. No one's gonna notice you get hit. Ah ha, ah ha ha ha ha!"

Oh, shit . . .

"Well now, how about getting this over with?" She giggled. "I've pulled out my knife. Want a nice, deep cut, starting in your head? Here goes!"

"Stop!"

A yell slipped out and I opened my eyes.

I saw Maya looking at me with her arms folded, and an infinite number of monsters.

She'd gotten me.

The knife had been a bluff.

And, stupid me, I'd opened my eyes.

"Tee hee! Just kidding about sending telepathy to everybody. Like anybody could do that."

Now I'd done it.

"I win, Mr. Wild Type."

Now that my eyes were open, they wouldn't close again. They were glued to the strange-looking monsters with saliva dripping from their jaws.

"These little guys . . . are going to devour your soul."

The monsters all jumped up at once.

Aiming for me.

They were going to eat me!

And just at that moment—

"Ahhhh" came a girl's scream.

Crash!

The sound of impact mixed with the squeal of tires and glass breaking echoed through the street.

"Ahhh-h!"

Maya's scream.

At the same time, the monsters disappeared into thin air.

I felt a little dizzy. When I opened my eyes, it was not the illusion, but reality unfolding before my eyes.

There I saw the source of the thunderous crash and impact.

One seriously damaged vehicle. For some reason, a small truck that had been driving on the main street had swerved off the road and had plunged into the alley where we were.

People were everywhere. Everyone was gathering around to see what had happened.

Maya had been knocked to the sidewalk when she tried to avoid the truck. She was groaning, holding her bleeding knee.

I was super, ultra lucky. Now was the perfect time to

get away. I ran off, not caring in which direction I was headed. I ran and ran and ran. And as I ran, I started to laugh. It was so strange I couldn't stand it.

Thinking about it before and after, though, it was no laughing matter.

As bystanders gathered and the sirens sounded, Maya decided to get away from the scene of the accident. Her skinned knee hurt, and she was mortified beyond belief. And in addition to the humiliation of being defeated on her first Psychic Patrol, she was afraid.

Who knew he'd turn out to be such a powerful psychic?

But he was . . .

"You failed, didn't you, Maya?"

Taken aback, Maya looked up and saw that Sho had been standing there. He was always showing up in front of people unexpectedly, and always with a face like haughtiness itself.

"I blew it. I didn't know that Ayano and the others would be with such a powerful psychic. That was naive," said Maya.

"That psychic caused that accident?"

"He did. And he's a Wild Type. He took a truck going down the street and made it come at me. Know what that means? He's a freak. He's incredibly powerful. He's telekinetic—he possesses psychokinetic power!"

"Did you say psychokinesis?" Sho's face twisted hatefully.

"We don't need him. No need to take him to the Greenhouse."

"Sho?"

"I'll go after him next. I will be the one who will make him disappear before the Farmers even know he exists."

As he said this, Sho disappeared like one of his own illusions.

I arrived at the pork bun shop where I told Ayano and the others we'd meet without knowing quite how I'd got there. Only I had for sure taken a big detour. I was covered with sweat. Ayano and Xiao Long had arrived a long time ago.

"What happened, Kakeru? Your face . . ." Ayano cried out when she saw my swollen lip.

"Did some delinquent beat you up?" asked Xiao Long. Not exactly, but pretty close. Now that I thought about it, that Maya chick did kind of look like one.

"No, worse. But what about you two? Where's Kaito?"

"It didn't work," said Xiao Long.

"I guess that's just how it is. I mean, that's his neighborhood. It might be better for Kaito to be there than to be with us," said Ayano.

"But even if he's there, the Farmers are bound to come find him someday. When they do, it does not matter how many ordinary drop-outs he's got with him, it will be absurd. They will capture him for certain."

"Oh, that's right, that's what I meant to tell you, your enemy's already here," I interjected.

"Huh?!"

"What did you say?!"

"Anyway, I don't want to just stand around talking. Shall we go in?"

"W-wait, what are you talking about? Don't tell me those injuries are—"

"Well, no, they are. You see, I met this girl called Maya and—"

"C'mere, Kakeru."

I tried to build a little suspense. Taking my arm fret-fully, the two led the way into the shop, looking around vigilantly.

As soon as I sat down, I began telling them every-thing that had happened to me while we'd been apart, with only a little embellishment.

At first they looked like they thought what I'd done was no big deal, but gradually their faces went pale and they fell silent. No sooner had I finished my story when, pulling me by the hand, they waved off the little old lady who'd come to take our order and left the shop.

"What's the rush about?"

"There's a terrible group of people after us. We have to get away from here this second."

"She's right. They're looking for the three of us right now," said Xiao Long.

"So they're looking for us, big deal. Like they're going to find us!" I scoffed.

"They'll find us!" he replied.

"We've got to get away!" finished Ayano.

Panting, we burst out of Chinatown, crossed under the freeway, and ran up to the top of a small hill, where there was a small park. Tree branches spread out widely overhead creating shadow, making us harder to see. We sat down on a park bench to catch our breath.

Almost out of breath, I asked the two of them, "Would you guys please stop dragging me around with-out any explanation? Why did we have to run out of there in such a hurry? And who is that girl? What do you mean, a terrible group of people? You mean that girl has friends who are just like her?"

"Where should I start?" said Ayano.

Taking a small mechanism about the size of a miniature radio out of his pocket, Xiao Long said, "Ayano, maybe we should start by explaining this."

I'd seen that mechanism before. It was what they had taken from that Farmer they'd beaten up back at that cabin.

"You're right. Xiao Long, will you please do the honors?"

"Huh? Me?"

"Yes, you. I mean, I don't even know much about the thing."

"Well, if you insist. But you *are* two years older than I am."

"Oh, geez. It doesn't matter which one of you explains it; just go for it, okay?" I urged Xiao Long, irritated. Reluctantly, he began.

"I'm so bad at this kind of thing. Jôi's smart. If he were here, he'd explain it in a way that's easy to understand. Okay, anyway, this mechanism is called a Seeker, and to sum it up in a few words, it's a machine thing used to detect psychics."

"A detector?! How can you can search for psychics with a machine?"

"You can, because psychics emit special brain waves, which this thing can pick up. It's hard to explain, so I'll just tell you what Jôi told me. There's this *huge* computer at the Greenhouse and it's networked to these Seekers. The characteristics of our brain waves are registered in the computer, and the Seekers and computer constantly exchange information."

I shivered.

Good God. That meant that unless the data was erased or the thing broken up, the Farmers could pursue them wherever they ran to.

No wonder they showed up wherever we went.

"A-and that girl who uses telepathy who attacked me?"

"I can tell you all about Maya," Ayano cut into the conversation. "That girl is mean and has a bad attitude! She sticks her nose in where she's not wanted. And she always has an evil expression in her eyes like a little doll, and she has *no* fashion sense. The Farmers ask her to buy our clothes, but all she ever gets is black. She's got terrible taste, like a crow or something . . ."

"Um, that's not what I meant."

"Oh, sorry. Maya's one of the Cultivated Types. And she's one of the elite Category Ones."

"Yeah, the kids who have mastered especially strong powers are the Category Ones, and the ones who are still undergoing training are called Category Twos. Category Threes have recognized aptitude, but their abilities are unknown," said Xiao Long.

"Okay, so that means you're Category Ones."

"Of course! Me, Xiao Long, Kaito, and also Jôi were Category Ones from the time we got to the Greenhouse. But Maya was originally one of those who just had aptitude. Her powers were cultivated. Before her ability surfaced, she was a coward, but then the second she became a great telepathist, she turned into a total bitch."

"Really, Ayano, I didn't need to hear that."

"Sorry, sorry. It's just that I can't stand her!"

This side of Ayano was so typically girly. No, maybe she was just being herself. Did that mean she was starting to trust me?

"Anyway, those guys Maya's always hanging around with are really dangerous. Some jerks named Sho and Takemaru." Ayano was writing the character for Shogun in the dirt with a dead branch to show me how to write the guy's name when it happened.

"That's enough out of you, blabbermouth."

"Huh?" That voice had suddenly come out of thin air in front of us.

At the same time something that looked like a person appeared from space.

Bam!

There was a sound like a balloon popping. Ayano was struck on the cheek.

"Ahh!" she screamed.

The sudden slap on the face knocked Ayano off the bench.

"Who's there?! Why did you—"

I was so angry that someone would hit a girl like that. Blood rushed to my head. I jumped up suddenly to grab that someone by the chest.

"You jerk!"

I heard Xiao Long's voice say "Kakeru, no!"

But I didn't stop. It was the first time I'd ever felt so angry. I had no time to feel scared. I was going to hurt anyone who would do that to Ayano. But despite my willingness to fight, my hands struck only at emptiness. The space there was empty again.

He disappeared?

Just as I thought that, someone hit me as hard as they could in the back of the head.

Fireworks exploded inside my head and I hit the ground. My nose hit, and sand got in my mouth.

"Huh? You're such a wimp." A voice came from above. A male voice.

"How can you be the same psychic who defeated Maya?"

He had a low and menacing voice, like a gang member.

For some reason he also seemed to have gotten the wrong impression. He thought I had psychic powers, too.

"Stand up, you!" came a shout.

My courage suddenly withered. It was no good, as I knew it would be.

That little burst of courage you get from anger can disappear in the blink of an eye. I wanted to just break down in tears and then apologize.

Sorry, I'm sorry, I'm really not psychic at all.

I don't know why Ayano has me twisted around her little finger, but I'm just an ordinary junior high school kid. I don't have any psychic ability, and I'm just a wimp, not the kind of person who would ever just go and pick a fight. Wimp—yes, that was the word that suited me best. Isn't that what those hooligans at school called me when I groveled in front of them? That was awful. Truly awful.

"Damn," I muttered.

The fire inside me was trying to start up again. This time it wasn't anger directed at my enemy. I was angry at myself. I couldn't forgive myself for wanting to just give up.

"Waaaaaa!" I got up. I dove at the feet of the guy looking down on me—or so I intended, but I missed again.

Why?

A boy with hair dyed brown and wearing a red sweater was floating in midair. He was floating about six feet above the ground, standing still with his arms folded.

Ayano and Xiao Long stood next to me in amazement as I gazed up, dumbfounded.

"Heh, what's wrong? Ayano, Xiao Long, why are you surprised, too? We're all from the Greenhouse. Even if you are just low-level idiots," said the boy with a cruel smile.

"Sho, when did you learn to float in midair?"

"Don't tell me you've been working toward psy-chokinesis?" said Ayano and Xiao Long simultaneously.

"Heh heh heh, well, since you're not that smart, I can see that's how it must look to you. This is a practical application of my strongest power, teleportation."

Teleportation—the ability to move from place to place in an instant. And then I understood why he had appeared in front of us so suddenly. Why he had disappeared the instant I went to grab him. And also why he was floating in midair.

"He's staying in midair by teleporting over and over, the jerk!" I said, pointing my finger.

The logic was simple. Why do images in cartoons look like they are moving? Because we see a series of static images moving little by little, which creates the illusion of movement. Sho was doing the same thing. I was sure what Sho was doing was teleporting upward just enough to compensate for the pull of gravity to make it look like he was floating in midair.

"Humph. It looks like *one* of you knows what you're doing. But I can't stand that you're not from the Greenhouse. And a Wild Type? You gotta be kidding."

It was a misunderstanding.

"Stand up, kid. Let's go man to man, a battle of the strongest."

Strongest . . .

An excessive assessment, to say the least.

But if this is what he was thinking, then maybe I could find a way to unexpectedly turn the tables on him.

Right, a bluff. For some reason it had worked before. I decided to see if I could pull off another one like the one that had been ended by chance with a car crash, allowing me to beat back Maya.

"You're on. I'll accept your challenge, but only if it's one on one." I stood up, bracing my trembling knees.

"It's no use! Don't do it! As you can see, he's not the normal kind of opponent."

"It's all right, just leave it all to me. I'm gonna show this guy my psychic powers."

I gave her a fearless smile. Ayano was perplexed. Which was understandable. They knew I was just a plain old ninth grader. There was no way I had any psychic powers. They didn't have the slightest idea what I was up to with this bluff, and they must have been totally confused.

But I did have a small chance. Maybe if I got lucky, I could knock this guy Sho out of the air as he did his repeated teleporting.

So I wanted them to join in on the bluff.

I put a lot of feeling into the look I gave Ayano and Xiao Long.

"Okay, this is going to be fun. Well, Telekineticist, come and get me. Show me that power you used to crash a car in front of Maya."

Ayano's and Xiao Long's eyes looked at me, their eyes wide when they heard Sho say that. Then they exchanged glances, and looked at me again, their faces filled with expectation.

Hey, whoa, you're not going to believe the same nonsense as this floating dork, are you?

That car crash was just a traffic accident, and I had just been lucky.

"All right, Kakeru, I'll place my bets on you," Ayano said, taking a step back.

"But I'll give you one piece of advice. He can only go about thirty feet every time he teleports."

Of course, thirty feet or three hundred, it was all the same to an ordinary person like me.

"Please be careful, Kakeru," Xiao Long said as he took a step back. "You must not let him touch you. The second you do, you'll be thrown thirty feet up in the air, and that will be the end."

Huh? I hadn't heard he could move other people besides himself.

"Ayano, Xiao Long, shut up! You small fry keep quiet and watch. If you so much as move a muscle, I'll kill you first!" said Sho.

"Fine, Sho. Xiao Long and I will stay out of it. But in exchange, don't do anything cowardly, like call any of your friends."

Huh, stay out of it? No way! If the bluff fell flat, I wanted them to jump into the battle.

"Heh heh heh, very well. Well now, shall we begin?" Saying this, Sho abruptly disappeared.

And then he reappeared in midair about twenty or thirty feet away and then disappeared again. As he repeated this, his appearing and disappearing picked up speed.

Pretty soon it looked as if there were lots of Shos. Furthermore, all of them were floating about six inches off the ground.

It was a strange sight. Like having a nightmare. Even though it was too late, I was regretting my stupid plan to pretend to have psychic powers.

There was no way I could fight him. What could I possibly do to a monster opponent like this besides throw the fistful of sand I'd snuck as I stood up?

Actually, I had planned to find some way to throw it in his face and make him close his eyes. If I did, maybe out of surprise Sho would stop his continuous midair teleporting for a moment. I thought that if he really was teleporting upward just enough to defy gravity, then if he couldn't do that for a second, then maybe he'd fall clumsily smack down to the ground.

It was an utterly unreasonable thought. No way could I hit him with grains of sand under these conditions. Now that I thought about it, why would he stay in just one place?

After all, this wasn't a game or something, it was a real battle, and my life was really in danger.

I was always daydreaming. At a time like this, if I was the me of my fantasy games, I would raise my legendary magic sword and cut down my enemy with the power of the Light.

I wanted a sword. I wanted power to take the place of a sword. I berated myself for not having it.

And the princess I was supposed to protect said she'd bet on me.

"Look out! Behind you!" Ayano cried out.

I turned around.

"Die!" Before my eyes I saw Sho's hand coming toward me to seize me.

"Waa!" I barely avoided him. His fingertips brushed my cheek. The leftover momentum in Sho's hand made him grab the woven iron trash can behind me. The trash can disappeared and reappeared in the sky a few seconds later before it came crashing down in the street in front of the park. The trash can jumped around in the street, pathetically smashed.

I shuddered. If that had been me, I'd be lying on the pavement covered with blood, with my head smashed in.

Sho flashed us an evil smile and floated back up to midair once again.

"Heh heh heh, good job dodging. Ayano saved you." He floated up slowly to a height of six inches off the ground. "But this time you won't escape." He made it sound like a question.

I had no time to lose. I had to do what I could. Whether it was a foolish bluff or something else, I had to throw this small bit of sand in my hand. I had to take aim. Flush with his success, maybe my opponent might get careless.

I did my utmost to show him a courageous smile. "Aren't *you* the one who had better run away?" I bluffed like crazy.

"What?" Sho's face went stiff.

"Last time with Maya, it was a car. You, I'm going to make a meteor hit you. There's a big stone falling out of the sky that's heading right at you. See?"

Startled, Sho looked up at the sky.

Now!

Aiming at Sho, I threw the sand in my hand as he looked toward the sky.

But I was a moment too late. Sho wasn't there anymore. Only a few feet away, but it was after he'd moved to the left.

"What are you trying to pull?" Sho was struck dumb by my worthless attack.

Both Ayano and Xiao Long looked at me in blank amazement, not knowing what was what.

I turned red not with fear but with embarrassment. I was so powerless.

Damn!

"Get down!!" I yelled, throwing some of the sand I had left in my palm at him one more time.

Even though I knew it wasn't going to work.

Just then . . .

Whoosh.

I felt a burst of wind pressure at my back.

And, without warning, a sudden strong gust of wind blew through the park.

The wind shook the trees and blew up sand that attacked Sho in midair.

Sand got in his eyes and Sho lost his balance. He fell and landed on the ground in a heap, just like a marionette whose strings had been cut.

"Let's get out of here!" I was running before the words were even out of my mouth.

Ayano and Xiao Long saw this and ran after me.

This was probably what running away as fast as your legs could carry you was like. To run, run, run, and run some more, without looking back. My opponent had psychic powers that would let him teleport thirty feet at a time. If we were even a second too late, that would be it. I didn't expect I was gonna be ultra, super lucky three times in a row. We ran through a small alleyway between private homes, cut through a vacant lot covered with weeds, and rushed into a thick copse of trees, not stopping until we were deep inside.

I stumbled and fell over a tree stump in the middle of the copse and collapsed.

Ayano and Xiao Long soon caught up.

The first words out of Ayano's mouth were, "You're amazing, Kakeru! You ran circles around Sho!"

"Huh? Ran circles around him? What are you talking about?" I said. This time Xiao Long shook me by the shoulders.

"You have psychic powers, too, Kakeru! That's what Jôi meant when he said 'Kakeru is one of us.' That you can use psychokinisis to manipulate wind is amazing!"

"Psy-psycho-ke . . . what?"

"Psychokinesis. The ability to move things around with your mind. It's concept power. That's the official name of the psychic power you can use."

"Oh . . . oh, no, really, let me explain, Xiao Long. It's just not true . . ."

Suddenly Ayano threw both her arms around my neck.

"Wh-why . . . Ayano . . ."

Ayano was in tears.

"Were you scared?"

"No, it's not that, I'm happy. I mean, I've met someone else like me who has psychic power. I'm so happy I could cry."

My heart went numb. Could this be? I was now the hero of my dreams, even if it was all a mistake. The princess whose life I'd saved clung to me and sobbed on my chest. How many times had I imagined this scene?

Somehow I just couldn't say it.

That I wasn't really a person with psychic powers. That my defiance before was only a bluff. That I'd only been able to fight Sho off because of a random gust of wind.

But this wasn't the right time to say it.

Or more accurately, I didn't feel like I wanted to confess. I'd admit everything later, after I'd calmed down, and that way I could be a hero for a little while.

But my moment of happiness didn't last.

"Ayano! Kakeru! Here they come again!" shouted Xiao Long as he sprung up.

Many shadows were approaching us from all directions. All of them advanced slowly, training guns on us.

"Geez, not even enough time to catch my breath!" In a fit of despair, I stood up and got ready to fight.

Even saying that I got ready to fight, it wasn't like a person pretending to have psychic ability could do anything, but for the time being I struck a pose with the others.

"Doesn't seem like there're any psychics. Just Farmers this time," said Xiao Long.

"How come they found us so easily?!"

"I told you, by following our brain waves with Seekers. So unless something changes, they'll find us quickly no matter where we run," Ayano said, taking the small stun gun she'd stolen from the Farmer out of her pocket and raising it.

"Well, then, how are we going to escape?" I asked, and Xiao Long said, "Jôi knows that, too."

"Jôi again? Tell me, what is his power?"

"I'll tell you if we get out of this alive!"

As we were talking, the Farmers began tightening their circle around us.

"What'll we do, Kakeru? There's more than ten of them! They might get us!"

In actuality, you had to leave me out. We only had two of us with real combat potential. This was more than just a bind. It was *hopeless*.

"Ayano, what about a mental projection? You could possess one of them like you did that other time," I said. Ayano shook her head.

"It won't be that easy. If there're this many of them, my physical body could be seized while I possessed one of them."

"Well, then, Xiao Long, how about with your *qigong*?"

"Impossible! Even if I could hit them at this distance, it's too far. It won't work unless they're a little closer."

"But we have something better, Kakeru, your psychokinesis! If you can make a car crash and control the wind, then taking care of all of those guys should be a snap, shouldn't it?" said Ayano.

"Well, see, that's what I've been meaning to tell y . . ."

I knew I should have been honest with them earlier.

Even if they were depending on me, it had only been a car crash and a natural phenomenon, not my powers or anything like that.

"Oh, no Kakeru! Hurry! The Farmers have guns!"

"But even if you want me to, there's nothing . . ."

"Everyone, ready, aim . . ." came a voice.

This was it! We were going to get shot!

"Fire!"

The sound of many shots rang out simultaneously.

"Argh!" Without thinking, I took cover.

Bam bam bam! The shots rang out around the tree we were hiding under. *Thunk, thunk.* Chunks of tree bark came down.

Somehow they'd missed us every single time.

"The Farmers are all sharpshooters. Don't tell me they missed . . ." this from Ayano.

"Wow, Kakeru, that was amazing!" said Xiao Long.

"You used psychokinesis to throw their aim off, didn't you?"

"Huh?"

They were reading too much into it. The Farmers just hadn't aimed well.

Again the command to shoot.

I wrapped my head in my hands and shut my eyes.

Just then, it happened.

"*Arrgh!*" a Farmer screamed.

At once I opened my eyes. There was a sea of flame.

A wall of flame surrounded us. But for some reason it didn't come near us. Instead it pursued the Farmers like a living thing. Some of the Farmers were rolling around on the ground, their clothes on fire.

"Wha-what is this? What on earth happened?"

"It's Kaito, Kakeru!" Ayano cried out with delight.

"Kaito? You mean that guy we—"

"Yes! Kaito's here, close by!"

"I knew Kaito would come!" said Xiao Long.

Then there was a voice from beyond the wall of flame. "Argh! Stop!"

"Shoot! Don't let them go!"

At the same time there was the roar of motorcycles. The wall of flame parted for a moment and four bikes jumped through.

Each one could hold two riders. Kaito was riding on the back on one of the luggage racks. "Get on, you three!"

"Kaito!" Ayano shouted. "You came! I knew you would!"

"We'll talk later. Just get on the bike!"

All three of us jumped on the back of the bikes Kaito had brought. With a roar of their engines and spewing up clouds of dirt, the bikes took off. I held on to the driver for dear life.

We shot out of the copse in a confusion of flame, gunfire, and engine noise. It had been a narrow escape.

Not long after we left with Kaito and his buddies on their bikes, the flames died down. The thicket wasn't that big. There wasn't that much to burn. That it had burned at all was due to Kaito's powerful incendiary ability as a psychoburner.

Even in the host computer at the Greenhouse, which stored information about people with psychic ability from all over the world, there were only twelve confirmed examples of people who could manipulate flame at will. Naturally Kaito was a Category One as well. He was an extremely rare and precious specimen.

Now that it was too late, Ikushima sighed at what an important commodity they had just lost.

"What a bunch of bunglers! Sheesh!" Ikushima shouted angrily at the group of Farmers under his command. "You should have been able to take the other two alive, even if you couldn't get Kaito! Ten of you missed your target on the first round of firing!"

"It was impossible, Ikushima-san." Ikushima turned around toward the voice. A youth lolled against a tree, smiling, hands thrust in his baggy chino pants. "Because if the opponent was a psychokineticist, then those guns might as well have been water pistols."

"Takemaru . . ." Ikushima unintentionally braced himself.

It was a necessary precaution. At any moment, Takemaru was willing to create total mayhem; he had never outgrown the mentality of the sort of small child who delights in pulling the legs off insects.

Ikushima had always disapproved of Takemaru's sense of mischief. He was always doing things like tripping passing Farmers by grabbing at their feet with invisible hands, and breaking all the lights in the hallway.

He was a small boy of fourteen, who, until arriving at the Greenhouse, had been bullied at school. The random acts of violence he perpetrated were probably a reaction to that awful time in his life.

"What do you mean, Takemaru? There was no one in the group who could use psychokinesis."

"Don't you see, Ikushima-san? There were Xiao Long, Ayano, and Kaito, who came to help them. But there was one more, wasn't there? A really ordinary-looking kid. Do you know what he is?"

"Now that you mention it, there was one more," Ikushima was frankly unsettled.

"A psychokineticist. What's more, he's an amazing

one, who easily got the better of Sho and Maya. Ha ha ha." Takemaru laughed pleasantly after he said this.

"You mean he's a Wild Type?"

"He must be. Because I don't think there's any other place besides the Greenhouse where they collect people like this and give them training."

"Great Scott! Then that's why the paralyzer guns we shot at them missed entirely!"

"That other psychic guy probably did it."

"Un-unbelievable. Even if they weren't live bullets, paralyzer bullets move at an initial speed of close to a hundred meters a second. It's difficult to concentrate on the concept of something moving far away under the best of circumstances, least of all when ten people shoot at the same time. If this person really did do that, then his or her power is of a different magnitude than anything we've seen before."

"Different magnitude?" Takemaru looked at Ikushima through lowered brows as he said this.

Now I've done it, thought Ikushima, hurriedly shutting his mouth tight. But it was too late.

Like a mischievous child, Takemaru stuck his tongue out at Ikushima, and facing the older man, began to focus his mind.

"C-cut it out, Takemaru. I'm not comparing the two of you. Sto—" By this time Ikushima was hanging upside down in midair.

"Arrgh! Put me down! All right, you're the best there is, Takemaru!"

"Don't hurt my feelings talking like that. I'll make you bang back and forth between trees like a pinball, Ikushima-san!"

Ikushima went up and down in midair like a yo-yo.

"Stop it!"

"You idiot! What are you doing?! Knock it off, Take-maru!"

At these words from Sho, who had teleported there, Ikushima fell to the ground.

"Hey there, Sho, what's with the angry look?" Take-maru was holding his sides as if it were really funny.

"How did you like this performance? I'm in especially good form today. How would the two of you like to fly in the sky? Oh yeah, want to go on a little flight to Yokohama, you, me, and Maya? It's okay, you can fly via teleportation, and I'll take care of Maya with my psychokinesis."

"Don't be ridiculous. It'd be a big deal if anyone saw us. We wouldn't get away with just a talking-to. We might even get punished by the Masquerade committee," Maya said, irritated.

"Ooh . . . ugh . . ."

Farmers rushed up to Ikushima, who moaned as he held his shoulder where he had been hit. "A-are you all right, Director Ikushima?!"

"Yeah, I'm fine." He stood up, braving the pain. If the dirt hadn't been soft, he might have broken bones. In his heart, Ikushima was quaking with fear. It was necessary to put a stop to the psychic's reckless actions with dignity. "I will be notifying my superiors of your bad behavior. You will not be getting any medication for a while."

"Huh?" The condescending, arrogant smile disappeared from Takemaru's face. Just like that. He was now so dependent on his medications that he couldn't function without them for even one day.

The medication given to him was not addictive, but he was under the impression that his abilities would disappear if his medication was cut off. Because of the defects in Takemaru's character, Ikushima-san had trained him to believe this in order to more easily control him. He had always been timid, and constant bullying had made his childhood a living hell. The psychokinesis he had gained through the medication was all that he had. What he was really addicted to was not the medication, but his own psychic power.

"Wait a minute, Ikushima-san. I was kidding just now. All I did was show off a little, right?!" Takemaru hurried toward Ikushima-san, who pushed him back.

"If you do not want to be punished, then do not mistake who your opponent is. If, as you say, a new Wild Type is acting with Ayano and the others, then capture him as well. And most important"—Ikushima took three capsules from his breast pocket and tossed them to the three of them—"Get Jôi back!"

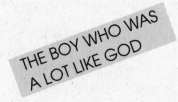

CHAPTER 5

THE BOY WHO WAS A LOT LIKE GOD

Riding two to a bike on the backs of Kaito's buddies' motorcycles, we went home.

When the four tricked-out bikes approached my school, Hiyama-san, who had come out to meet us, opened the gate with a look of amazement.

It was a good thing that it was Golden Week; no school clubs were doing activities at school. Had any students or teachers been there, they would have made something of a fuss about a motorcycle gang descending on the school.

Maybe they looked like a bunch of low-down cheap punks, with their bleached-blond hair and multiple piercings, but we owed them our lives. When we got off the bikes, they apologized for their earlier insolence.

"Sorry about what happened. If we'd known you were friends of Kaito's we wouldn't have made fun of you. I swear. I mean, really, it's not like we did anything. It's just that it's so weird to see such normal-looking people around there, so we had to say hi, you know?"

At first, I'd thought they were a bunch of scumbags.

But now that they were clapping me on the back and apologizing, they didn't seem like such bad guys after all.

"Yeah? I wonder about that," remarked Kaito. The guys laughed uneasily.

"Wa ha ha ha, it's true, Kaito."

"He's right. So to make it up to you, we brought you here on our bikes."

"Give us a break, huh? I mean, we're the ones who got hurt."

I wasn't sure if they were even old enough to have driver's licenses, but I think they were older than Kaito. Still, Kaito was indisputably their leader; they relied on him. When it was finally time to part, everyone was teary-eyed and sniffling.

That's right, instead of going back to his home and his friends, Kaito had chosen to stay and fight with Ayano and the others from the Greenhouse.

"Well, now, I think I'll pay Jôi a visit." As Kaito walked through the school gate, he looked a little lonely. He did not turn around to watch his friends leave, his shoulders set with steely determination: he had resolved to win freedom by fighting the Farmers.

"Hey! You with the big tits, where's Jôi at?" he said rudely. In the next moment, he got a sound *thwok* on the forehead.

"Uwah! What'd you do that for?"

"Kid, that's no way to talk to a lady. My name is Hiyama. And don't forget the 'san.'"

Even a tough guy like Kaito was no match for Hiyama-san. "I'm sorry," he said, bobbing his head in apology, hand pressed to his injured forehead.

I very nearly laughed, and Kaito glared at me. "Hey brat, don't laugh. If you do, I'll punch you out."

That earned him another blow from Hiyama-san.

"Ow! What, again?"

"He's not a brat. His name is Kakeru. Kids these days don't have any manners. You better learn everyone's names quick. You're going to be spending a lot of time with them."

"All-all right. It's Kakeru. Kakeru."

Kaito faced me and offered his right hand. "Nice to meet you, psychokineticist. I heard about you from Ayano earlier. You beat the shit out of Maya and Sho, didn't you?"

"Huh? Beat the shit out of? Well, I mean, uh, let me explain," I hemmed and hawed.

It looked like the tale was getting bigger and bigger.

What to do? It looked like there was no backing out now.

"Huh? Kakeru has psychic powers? Seriously?" from Hiyama-san.

Right! Hiyama-san could explain it for me. Anyway, if this misunderstanding wasn't taken care of, then things could get pretty out of hand.

"I've been meaning to talk to you about that, Hiyama-san, actually I . . ."

"Yes, Hiyama-san, he is!"

Ayano leaned forward to interrupt. "He was totally amazing! First he took on this telepathist named Maya and fought her off with a car crash, then right in front of us he called up some wind to drive off this guy named Sho who can teleport, and then last, when the Farmers had us cornered, he deflected all the bullets from their paralyzer guns. He saved our lives."

She'd beaten me to the punch. I could only smile.

Hiyama-san looked dubious, and I didn't contradict her when she murmured gently into my ear, "Well, I supposed it's okay, Kakeru. You wanted to try to protect the princess, didn't you?"

"Hiyama-san! What are you saying?!"

She gave a sharp, knowing laugh. "Well, kiddies, let's go. I made dinner already." Laughing loudly, Hiyama-san led the way across the school grounds.

We entered the janitor's room that was Hiyama-san's home, and a delicious smell tickled our noses. Stew bubbled away over low heat on a portable gas burner.

Jôi was still sleeping on the futon. Hiyama-san had made a makeshift bed out of a bunch of floor pillows. It was so like Hiyama-san, who was kind of a slob, to just leave the pillows out on the floor like that.

Kaito went to Jôi's side, and clucking his tongue, said, "You said everyone was going to survive and jumped into the river first. That's why you're in the shape you're in. Idiot. Now what'll you do?" His words were gruff, but that was just his usual manner. You could tell he was really worried. He questioned Hiyama-san insistently about what she had fed Jôi and how she kept him hydrated.

Hiyama-san brought the stew she had made on the portable gas burner to the low eating table, while we laid out the dishes and set the table.

"Okay, everybody, dig in and help yourselves," said Hiyama-san. Just as she was handing out disposable chopsticks, Kaito went straight for the meat, earning himself a nice *thwok* on the forehead from Hiyama-san.

Xiao Long and I both burst into laughter as we noticed we were avoiding the onions. It looked like I'd found a friend in hating onions.

Ayano turned out to be a girl with a healthy appetite. She would always collide with Kaito when she reached out with her chopsticks to take some meat, and then they would do paper, rock, scissors to see who got some

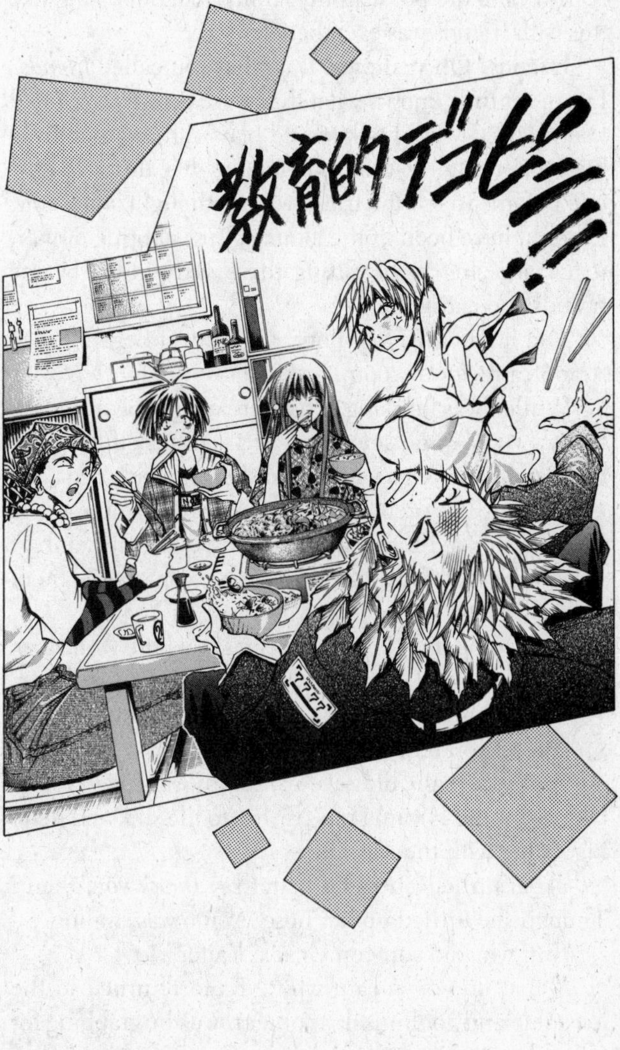
教育的デコピン!!!

first. Somehow Ayano always won, and, as the loser, Kaito had to settle for a piece of tofu instead.

It was an enjoyable dinner. It was fun to eat stew directly out of the pot with my family, too, but eating like this with friends was even better.

Friends? Oh yeah, was this what you called *friends*? I've never truly known what they were before now. I had had friends I would talk to and play with at lunchtime, but I'd never felt a sense of belonging like this with anyone before. To tell the truth, when I thought about how I should have been home alone eating a boring dinner, it felt amazing to be sitting there surrounded by my friends and eating stew.

And it had only been one day since it began. Since Ayano came to my room.

While I was thinking about this and giving my chopsticks a rest, Ayano stood and excused herself from the table and went to go wash the dishes she had used.

"Whew, I'm pretty full. Hey, Ayano, do mine while you're at it," said Kaito, dumping his own in the sink.

"You've got a lot of nerve, don't you. Wash them yourself. Geez."

"Aw, come on. I just saved your life a little while ago, remember?"

"Oh, so now you're going to *demand* gratitude?"

"Aren't you feisty? Christ!"

"But you really did save us, Kaito," said Xiao Long, taking my and Hiyama-san's dishes to the sink and helping Ayano with the washing.

"That's true. Guess I'd better say *thank you*, then." Though she turned up her nose, Ayano was smiling.

"But why did you come back, Kaito?"

"What do you mean, why?" Kaito returned to the low table and got himself another *thwok* by grabbing for Hiyama-san's cigarettes.

"I'm asking why you came back here from the Nationless Quarter where your friends are," Ayano asked in a voice loud enough to be heard over the faucet.

"Well, Ayano, that's because *you're* here, of course."

Ayano was stonefaced at Kaito's attempt at humor. "I'm serious. If you're just forcing it, you'll regret it later."

"Don't be stupid. I'm not forcing anything." Perhaps to hide his embarrassment, Kaito flopped down faceup on the tatami. "Well, okay, maybe I didn't think you guys could make it on your own."

"But if you didn't think you could leave us alone, aren't those other guys the same?"

"Well, yeah."

"Well, then . . ."

"The gang may not have had much of a life while I was gone, but you guys were even worse off. You'd be caught and taken back there pretty quickly, or maybe killed. So, I figured, if there are friends I can't leave on their own, it's you guys."

"Kaito . . ."

"So that's why. So we're still friends."

"Thank you."

"Fool. Why couldn't you have just said that in the first place?!"

"Ayano, you've rinsed it clean," said Xiao Long, taking the dish she'd been holding under the running water for some time. "Now we've got Kakeru, another powerful friend. All we need to do is wait for Jôi to wake up."

"I guess," said Kaito.

The question of whether I was really powerful aside, it was clear that everybody believed everything would go better when Jôi woke up. Maybe they were going to tell me what Jôi's ability was if we escaped from that attack by the Farmers unscathed.

To indirectly approach that topic, I asked Hiyama-san, "How is Jôi doing?"

"Dunno. I know a little about both Western and Eastern medicine, but I've never seen or heard of a condition as strange as this. His pulse beats only twenty times per minute. Only one third as often as that of a healthy person. His body temperature is only ninety-four degrees."

"Ninety-four degrees? Isn't that incredibly low?"

"Yeah, it's low. It'd be dangerous if it kept going down, but if it's stable it's kind of like hibernation."

"Hibernation? Maybe it's psychic sleep!" Ayano interrupted.

"What's that?" I said.

"Ikushima-san said that sometimes very powerful psychics go into a state similar to hibernation to recover their strength. It's called 'psychic sleep.' If that's what Jôi's doing, I'm sure there's nothing to worry about." Ayano looked relieved.

"Ikushima-san? Who's that?"

"Um. One of the leaders of the Farmers at the Greenhouse. He had quite an interest in us, especially in Jôi's ability."

It was the perfect opening to ask about Jôi's ability. I wasted no time in asking.

"What is Jôi's ability? Tell me about it now."

"All right, but don't freak out, Kakeru."

"I've freaked out enough already just over your power, y'know."

"Um hm. But this is special. I mean, Jôi's power is—"

"Prescience." Kaito interrupted. "There are other people who have abilities like psychometry, who can read minds or who can see things with their eyes shut.

What's special about Jôi's power is that he has the power to see the future. Prescience."

"P-prescience, huh?" That was my honest impression. Not the answer I'd expected. I'd thought they were going to say he had some more terrible, amazing power. The word *prescience* was something even I knew, and in the world of science fiction was pretty common.

"Prescience!!" shouted Hiyama-san loudly from where she sat next to me as I was thinking this. "Seriously? Hey!" and grabbed Kaito's shirt. Kaito, who was nearly six feet tall, shrank back.

"Uh, yeah. Seriously."

Maybe using force wasn't that feminine, but it was still completely in character for Hiyama-san. I wondered what she'd done before she'd started working here. I was pretty sure she'd been something else besides a handyman at a junior high school.

"It was Jôi's prescience that allowed us to escape from the Greenhouse," said Xiao Long.

"How good is the probability that's he's right? That boy, Jôi, how good are the odds that his predictions are going to be right, Xiao Long?" Hiyama-san was in a state of excitement. I wonder why?

"He hits the target every time, of course. I mean, if he wasn't they wouldn't call it prescience, would they?"

"Which means one hundred percent." With that, she put a cigarette in her mouth and sank into thought.

I asked her, "What's wrong, Hiyama-san? Is it such a marvel?"

This is really what I thought. If you were going to marvel at something, Ayano's out-of-body projection left me much more amazed.

"You don't get it, do you, Kakeru?"

"Huh? Get what?"

"You don't understand at all what prescience that is correct one hundred percent of the time is. That's why you can just sit there so nonchalantly."

I was taken aback.

"Kakeru, you don't get it, do you, what a terrible thing it is to know the future. Suppose Jôi tells you that tomorrow you're going to die. Could you stand it? Tomorrow would be okay, because you'll know pretty quickly one way or another if it's going to happen. Suppose it's some day next year? Then that entire year leading up to that day would be hell."

I tried imagining myself in that position. I felt my spine grow cold. No doubt I would think the sound of a clock ticking would sound like the sound of footsteps going up the stairs to the gallows.

You're going to die in one hour, so what would happen in those final ten, five, one minutes? Shaking with fear, nevertheless unable to go against fate and save your own life, you would fall into despair.

Everyone has thought they wanted to know the future at one time or another. But they only want to know because deep down, they believe the future will be pretty good. The truth is that you only have a few big events to look forward to in your future, then lots of ordinary stuff, and, finally, the one event that destroys you.

Ayano saw me go pale at Hiyama-san's words and said, "It's okay, Kakeru. When I met Jôi, I thought the same thing, but it's not like that. He doesn't understand stuff to that extent. He only understands the kind of future that heralds big change up to right before the event starts, but not the outcome of the event itself."

"The future that changes fate?"

"Yes. This, for example. Say you've got a deck of cards. Say you shuffle them well and pick some cards in order. After that, if you open an envelope where Jôi wrote down his prediction of what cards you would pick in what order, he would be right."

"R-really? Not just some hocus-pocus sleight of hand?"

"I hear there's a sleight-of-hand trick that's similar, but Jôi's is different. He would really know. He's always right about stuff like this."

"W-wow! If he can do that, doesn't he already know everything?"

"It's not like that. According to Jôi, even if he knows it, it's not the important stuff, and he doesn't understand it completely."

"He can see the future without completely understanding it?"

"Yes. I mean, that's how it is, isn't it? I mean, no matter what card you pick, do you think it would cause your doom?"

"I'm pretty sure it wouldn't."

"Sure. Jôi says he can see right through almost all that kind of future. But he can't see the kind of future where, like, if you get on a certain plane, you're going to die. In cases like that it seems like he sees scenes from the future like the plane crashing, or that the person who was supposed to get on did not for some reason, at the same time."

"Now that you mention it, there isn't anyone who would get on a plane if they knew it was going to crash. Oh, but what about something like this? For example, if someone who heard that prediction tells someone else who is supposed to die on the plane . . ."

"If something like that were to happen, Jôi wouldn't be able to see that future. It's like it's behind a locked door. He can't go there."

In other words, taking their escape from the Green-house as an example, it meant that he had seen images of them surviving their jump into the river. When I thought about it that way, I finally understood Jôi's ability.

To sum it up, Jôi only had the power to know the future, but not the power to change it. He could only predict the future that his predictions had already had some kind of effect on. There was no doubt that his ability had a fundamental difference in weight from that of the other psychics I'd met in the last two days.

Just to take one example: if, for some reason, all of mankind was going to be annihilated tomorrow as the result of some inevitable event, then Jôi would be able to predict that horrible, unchangeable future.

"I see. Just barely avoiding a time paradox. In a certain sense, that makes Jôi's ability more believable," said Hiyama-san, giving Jôi's sleeping face a penetrating look.

"What's a time paradox?" Kaito asked. I guess he'd never read a science fiction novel.

"Say someone goes back in time and kills their own grandfather. Then he would never have been born, and therefore he can't go back and kill his own grandfather, right? That's what they call the kind of paradox that would inevitibly arise if anyone were actually to use a time machine."

"But, hey, with predictions and premonitions, it's not like you're going to use a time machine to go back into the past."

"It's the same thing. What happens if someone knows, thanks to a premonition, that in the future a certain person is going to kill them, so they go and kill that person first? Then the future where they were going to be killed is changed, and the prediction turns out to be wrong."

"Hmm, I see. It's kind of complicated, I guess." Kaito said, shaking his head in puzzlement.

That Jôi's predictions were one hundred percent accurate meant that he couldn't foresee the future touched by this time paradox in the first place, but . . . maybe he could see it after all. He just wasn't telling anybody. Doubts began to simmer.

If he knew everything, but didn't tell anyone, then the boy called Jôi was a lot like God.

Always watching, always knowing the glory and catastrophe of the future. Isn't that just like the fate of Jesus Christ, who knew all the while that there was a traitor among the apostles at the Last Supper, and accepted the fate of dying on the cross so he could be resurrected after death?

Jesus?

That's right. I wonder if Jesus had known that the atomic bomb would be dropped on Hiroshima. How that would kick off the proliferation of nuclear bombs that could destroy the world many times over. Or if he had already seen the day when the human race would perish.

The words *Judgment Day* came to mind.

It couldn't be . . . could it?

I felt a cold that knew no end as I looked at Jôi's angelic, sleeping face.

So we'd eaten, drunk, and been merry. Next thing I knew, we'd all fallen asleep in a heap in the small janitor's room. I dozed off, and later opened my eyes to find Kaito's great big feet right in front of my face.

"Oh, geez . . ." I brushed them away as I got up.

Someone had turned off the lights and the room was in total darkness.

I got up with the intention of going to the bathroom, and headed over there, being careful not to step on anybody.

Ayano was close to the exit. I could see her expression, lit by the light coming in through the small window in the door from the emergency exit sign in the hallway. She looked like a sleeping child. All the psychics, even Xiao Long, looked very grown-up for their ages, but their faces looked childlike when they slept.

Truthfully, I wanted to watch her sleep, but if she woke up, she'd think I was up to something and I didn't want that, so being careful not to make any noise, I crept out of the room.

The lights in the hallway were turned off. I had just the light from the moon and the emergency exit to guide me. Without students or teachers, the school felt really big.

And too quiet. My footsteps echoed, and I could even hear the echo of my own breathing. The hallway stretched on straight like a hospital corridor. It was somehow eerie. The bathroom was on the opposite side of the hallway from the janitor's room.

After I took care of what I was there to do as quickly as possible, I hurried down the hall.

"Hu hu . . ." I felt a presence stifling a laugh in the depths of the stagnant dark hallway.

I stopped and looked hard. No one was there. Well, why would there be? It was almost one in the morning. No one but us would come to school at this time.

"Heh, heh, heh . . ." I started walking again, but this time I heard the laughter more clearly.

Someone was here, no doubt about it. At the end of the hall in front of the bathroom. I couldn't be sure because there was no light from the emergency exit sign there and it was dark, but I was sure that a shadow, shaped something like a person, was crouched there.

I stopped and called out, "Is anybody there?"

At this, the fluorescent lights by the sink in the hallway flickered before turning on.

The shape rose up in the cold, white light.

It was a boy. A thin, small boy. My flesh crawled. He wasn't a student here. Definitely not. He had to be another psychic.

And just as I was about to run—

Crash!

The glass in the hallway windows exploded with a sound that pierced through my ears.

"Arrgh!" I threw myself on the floor, the glass shards raining down on me.

There was no doubt about it. He was definitely the enemy—the third assassin, let loose to capture Ayano and the others.

"Ayano! Xiao Long! Kaito! Hiyama-san! Wake up, wake up!" I yelled as I crawled down the hall full of glass.

"A psychic! The enemy is here!" I said, and looked over my shoulder. I'd expected there to be between a hundred feet or so between us, but he was coming at me unbelievably fast. He wasn't running. He was floating in midair. Still crouching, he flew down the hall.

"Arrgh!" I ran for dear life. The glass snapped and popped under my feet.

If I slipped and fell, I'd get all cut up by the glass shards. But I had no time to worry about that now.

I had to let everyone know! I had to tell them!

"Wait, Wild Type." He came after me as I untangled my feet as quickly as I could and started to run again. Then he floated down right in front of me and blocked my path.

Hands in his pockets, he flashed me a lunatic grin. "You, what's your name?"

Shocked, I answered, "Ka-Kakeru."

"Humph. Kakeru, huh? How do you write it?"

"The 'sho' character from the 'hisho' that means 'flight' . . . but y'know . . ." This was bad. This guy really was dangerous. I felt as if he was different from the two that I'd already met. I could tell he was more irrational, less predictable.

"Kakeru, eh? My name's Takemaru. The 'ju' from 'moju' for 'ferocious beast,' and the 'maru' that means 'circle,' as in the shape, make Takemaru. Nice name, isn't it? Nice and strong. I really, really like it. I used to hate it, though."

"Wh-why did you used to hate it?" Ayano and the others must have woken up. At least Hiyama-san would be awake. I mean, she was the school watchman and everything.

I had to stall for time.

"That's such a cool name. Why did you hate it?"

In response to my question, Takemaru let his smile fade. "Because I was bullied."

"Huh?"

"They bullied me a lot because here I had this strong name and I was small and weak. It started when I was in elementary school."

"R-really? That must have been tough." I regretted it as soon as I'd said it.

"Tough?" Takemaru looked at me with a frown. I knew it. I'd gotten him angry.

"Oh, it was *tough*, believe me. They stole everything I had. When I put my shoes in the cupboard, they always got thrown away and I had to start taking them with me into the classroom."

What a sad story. But at my school there were certainly one or two people like that.

"The saddest part was when I went to stay overnight

at the School of the Sea mobile classroom, or whatever it was called. I always woke up in the restroom, where they'd left me. They used to put weird stuff in my food, too."

"Wh-what do you mean by 'weird stuff'?"

"Cockroaches and stuff. Ah ha ha."

It was not something to laugh about. I'd never heard of anything so awful in my whole life.

"They hit me every day, but I got used to it. What was really hard was when they made me do dirty stuff, or when they told me to do embarrassing stuff in front of everyone." Remembering was bringing tears to Takemaru's eyes.

As you might expect, I had to sympathize a little bit, but after hearing the next part of the story, my sympathy went with the bullies.

"But then one day it changed. Little Takemaru was on the platform at the station. The leader of the bullies, let's call him 'A,' took all my pocket money. Oh, yeah, I forgot to say that the junior high I was going to was part of my private elementary school. I had to take the train to get there. Oh, sorry for getting off topic there. Heh heh heh." Takemaru's smile was back, a much more brutal smile than before.

Wasn't anyone awake yet? Wake up, already! This crazy guy was going to freakin' kill me.

"Then it happened. For some reason, 'A' fell right onto the train tracks, was badly injured and almost died. The other students on the platform who saw what happened said Takemaru pushed him off, and Takemaru got sent to a facility for troubled kids. But Takemaru didn't actually lay a finger on 'A.' Yet somehow, 'A' floated up and was blown onto the tracks by a wind that wasn't there."

Ayano, Xiao Long, Kaito, Hiyama-san, come on! I prayed in earnest.

"Takemaru came to the attention of the Farmers in that facility. Then Takemaru happily went to live in the Greenhouse and used the power he obtained there to get the revenge he deserved, on all the kids who had bullied him. The end. Heh heh heh! Well, that's my life story. Like it?"

"What do you mean, 'the revenge he deserved'?"

"I'm sure you know what I mean. No one acknowledges that psychic powers even exist, so no matter what I do, it's not illegal. So, I asked the Farmers to let me practice my combat skills on the kids from school." Takemaru laughed gaily as he said this.

Yeah, he was as nutty as a fruit cake.

"A-and what happened to them, those kids who bullied you?" I just had to ask.

"Hmm. I wonder. Heh heh heh."

A number of sad scenarios went around in my head. I thought Takemaru was a psychokineticist. Someone with psychic powers who could really use psychokinesis—the very power that everyone believed I had.

If so, he could do whatever he wanted to people with "unseen hands." It would be child's play to make someone jump in front of a speeding car or fall in front of a train. Or he could lift them way up into the sky, only to let them drop. Or make a rope wrap itself around their necks. Or this, that, and the other awful thing, all without laying a finger on anyone.

That could very well be my own fate at any moment. I wanted to break down into tears and apologize.

As if he were the kind of guy to just let things go this time if you apologized.

"Well, now, shall we get started, Kakeru? This is a

contest to see whose power is stronger, yours or mine. Heh heh heh."

I was abruptly assailed with a sensation like vertigo. But I soon knew that vertigo was not what it was. The sensation of my body weight that I felt in my legs abruptly vanished. In the next instant, my body was floating in midair. I couldn't feel anything stringing me up. I drifted in midair, feeling more like I was floating in water.

"Uwah! Put me down!"

Takemaru laughed, amused, as he watched my legs flail about.

"Ah ha, ah ha ha ha ha. My goodness, what a sight. Can this be the psychokineticist who got the better of Sho and Maya?"

I told you I wasn't! I was just your everyday average ninth grader, not a psychokineticist or anything like that. I'd just gotten to know Ayano and the others through a series of random incidents. I wanted to bawl that I had beaten Sho and Maya because of good fortune that you might get once or twice in your lifetime, but managed to hold myself back. Thinking all the while that if he knew that, Takemaru might throw me against the wall like a toy he no longer wanted. That's the kind of opponent this crazy psychic was.

So I decided to put all my strength into pretending to be tough in order to buy some time, just like I had before.

I only prayed that Ayano and the others would get here soon.

"Leave it at this, Takemaru! Otherwise I will be forced to show you the true depth of my power!" But my toughness backfired.

"Yeah? That sounds like fun. Hurry up and show me what you've got. Well, come on! Now!" Takemaru's voice echoed down the hallway. All the while he was swinging my body like a yo-yo.

This was it. I was going to die. I'd be thrown against the wall and burst open like a tomato.

It happened just in that moment.

Whoosh.

Gigantic flames that reached the ceiling broke out in the school hallway where there was nothing to burn, throwing up a curtain between Takemaru and me.

Instinctively Takemaru jumped back and used his powers to stay in midair. I dropped to the ground like we'd changed places and hit the floor.

"Yo, Takemaru, my friend, thanks for your hospitality," came a deep, threatening voice from behind.

There stood Kaito, hands thrust into the pockets of his black jeans.

I was so happy I could have cried. I felt I had been saved. But contrary to how I felt, Kaito was stiff with fear. It seemed that even Kaito, who had the power to conjure up a sea of flame in a hallway, needed to steel himself for a battle with Takemaru.

"Sorry that was such a close one, Kakeru. But it's just too dangerous to go after Takemaru head on." Kaito made a gesture with his chin, and the flames abruptly went out like in a magic show.

"It's okay, Kaito. Good luck." I got up, holding my aching behind where it had hit the ground. Blood dripped from my hand; it had been cut by the fallen glass.

"Don't say that. You're a psychic, too. How about a little demonstration of the power you used to twist Sho and Maya around your little finger?"

I didn't like that I couldn't just say "Sure thing!"

"Humph. Where are the other three, Mr. Psychoburner?" asked Takemaru, giving a confident smile.

"You mean me?" Ayano appeared on the opposite side of the hall. She held a paralyzer gun. Looked like she'd taken the stairs up to the second floor and come down on the other side so they could attack Takemaru from both sides.

"Freeze, Takemaru. One move and I'll shoot."

Takemaru wrinkled his nose in a hateful sneer. "You think you could hit me with that thing, Ayano? Psychokineticists can easily make paralyzer guns miss their target."

"Think so, huh? We're not close to you, and in opposite directions. Could a Cultivated Type like you pull off a stunt like using your psychokinesis on both of us at once?"

Takemaru sank into sullen silence.

"The second you use your power on Kakeru and Kaito, I'll shoot you with this paralyzer!"

"That's right! If you focus your mind on Ayano and try to do something, I'll make you into a ball of fire."

I see. I figured out why they had split up.

With the broken hall windows at his back, Takemaru had been halted by Ayano's and Kaito's strategy of putting him in the middle.

"Hah, what's wrong, Takemaru? Can't you focus? All we did was split up. Looks like it's true that even if Cultivated Types have strong power, they can't think outside the box."

So Takemaru was the Cultivated Type of psychic, one whose powers had been aroused through the use of medication and machines. On the one hand, they could focus strong power, but it looked like they couldn't focus their minds when the target was split into two like this.

"In my case and in Kaito's, we've been psychics for as long as we can remember. Using our psychic powers is as easy as using our hands and feet, but I guess it's not like that for you, Takemaru."

"You guys whose powers were awakened with drugs are like babies with guns. Even if you can pull the trigger, it's still at least ten years before you'll know what you're doing. Now beat it and go home with your tail between your legs. If you do, we'll let it slide this time."

"If you think the three of you can treat me like this, you're making a big mistake," Takemaru said—and jumped out of the broken window.

"Always has to have the last word." Kaito pursued Takemaru to the window and was about to lean out. Without warning, someone appeared as if they'd gushed out of the dark night and punched Kaito in the face.

"Ungh!" Kaito grunted as he was thrown down the hall.

Whoever the attacker was, he disappeared, only to reappear unexpectedly in the hallway a moment later. He looked down at Kaito, on the floor of the hall, holding his hand to his face, and laughed at him. "Heh heh heh, guess you shouldn't talk so big, Kaito." It was Sho, the teleporter.

"Wh-why *you*!" In a moment Sho was surrounded by Kaito's angry flames.

"Tch!" Sho teleported. But when he reappeared a few feet away, smoke puffed up from the edges of his sleeves.

Shaking off the flames, Sho said, "You're pretty good there . . ."

"I'll turn you into a ball of fire, Sho!" His face livid, Kaito sent forth more flames.

However, Sho teleported again, this time perfectly. "You think you can catch me that easily, Kaito?!"

The red sweater Sho wore appeared, visible in the dark hallway only because of the light of the emergency exit sign, and then disappeared like a blinking light. Kaito's flames gleamed, as if in pursuit.

A nightmare of a psychic battle was unfolding before my eyes. All I could do was watch, and then wait for the outcome.

"Kaito, step back! I'll get him via mental projection!" said Ayano, shutting her eyes and starting to focus her mind.

But just then . . .

"Aghh!" Ayano fainted in agony, holding her ears.

Ah ha ha ha. Look at you, Ayano came a girl's voice. What's more, I didn't hear it in my ears, but directly inside my head.

I'm indebted to you for last time, Kakeru. Right now, Ayano's got heavy metal music, which she hates, turned up to full volume inside her head. Tee hee.

Apparently even the telepathic Maya was nearby.

Well, now, Kakeru, you're next. I have a really fantastic hallucination for you.

No sooner were the words out of her mouth, then the hallway suddenly overflowed with decaying zombies.

"Arrrgh!" The hair all over my body stood up from terror.

The attacking zombies tore at my body. The fear of death burned in my chest.

Even though I knew they weren't real, my natural instinct to escape made me start to lose consciousness.

I felt faint.

No, Kakeru, you must not let her win!

A voice that wasn't Maya's was inside my head.

It's me. Ayano. Shut your eyes. I will move your body.

Mental projection. Ayano was inside my body. I shut my eyes, like she told me.

As the zombies receded, I felt as if my body went

away. For just a few seconds my senses of sight and hearing, and the feeling of even having a body, disappeared completely. When they came back, I had already run out of the school building and was crouched down in the school garden.

When I opened my eyes, I saw Ayano's transparent form as she left my body.

"Ayano, what about the zombies?"

It's okay. They won't come here. Maya is a Cultivated Type of psychic, so she can't use her telepathy on anyone this far away from her.

"B-but . . ."

Leave Maya to me. I'll find her while I'm projecting, move into her, and punish her.

Saying this inside my head, Ayano left my body and flew up into the pitch-black sky.

"Arrrrgh!"

Regaining consciousness, I screamed and started to run. I had to get out of there. No way could I possibly fight those guys. What could a plain old ninth grader like me do in a nightmare like this? I ran without looking back.

When I came out of the back garden, I found myself in front of the old wooden gymnasium, which was being demolished. I went over the fence, on which "Danger of collapse. Do not enter" was written in big letters, forced open the door that had a broken lock, and went inside.

I would hide in here until the battle of the psychics was over. It was the only thing to do. I pushed a vaulting horse in front of the door to block the entrance.

My shoulders lowered in relief as I sank to my knees. Then a voice came from behind me, as if someone had been waiting for me to do just that. "Nice. It's quiet here. Perfect for a one-on-one contest."

Startled, I turned around.

There, in the pitch-black gym, on that wooden floor with the broken slats, sat Takemaru, his arms wrapped around his knees. "I had Sho teleport you here. Convenient, isn't it, to have friends like that?" Takemaru stood up unsteadily. "Thanks to Sho, my delectable prize didn't get away." He laughed with pure delight.

Yeah, this was as bad as it could possibly get.

This time, I might really get killed.

And Ayano and Kaito were probably fighting as hard as they could against Sho and Maya.

Right! Where was Xiao Long? What about Hiyama-san?

I had no time to worry about where they were or what they were doing. Soon my body was flying toward the gym's basketball hoop like it had been thrown by the invisible man.

Meanwhile, Akira Hiyama and Xiao Long had left the school building and moved Jôi to the storage shed in the corner of the garden. They were going to take the still-unconscious Jôi to a good hiding place before joining the fight.

"Okay. Let's go back, Xiao Long." Hiyama-san laid Jôi down on the gym mat she had carried on her shoulders.

"I agree. Let's be quick. I don't think Ayano and Kaito can be defeated very easily by those drug addicts, but we need to get this over with and get out of here. Now that they've found us, the Farmers can't be far behind," and just when Xiao Long opened the door of the shed . . .

Smack!

A dull, explosive sound.

Before he could yell, Xiao Long was flung onto his back and knocked unconscious.

"Xiao Long!" Hiyama-san was about to go over to him when she saw the armed men approaching and promptly hid herself in the shadows.

"Damn! Too late," Hiyama-san cursed her own carelessness.

They'd been here all along, brought by the psychics pursuing Kakeru, and waited for Ayano, Kaito, and the rest of us to get separated before they struck.

To think she hadn't anticipated that easy trick. "Guess I'm a little slow on the uptake."

She had never missed basic training, and that left her confident. However, she had changed from when she had belonged to a certain governmental organization and had faced danger every day on the front lines. It had been three years since she'd left her job for some unspecified reason, and she probably should have been aware of how rusty her ability to sense danger had become.

She checked the remaining paralyzer gun in her hand.

The weapon was delicately made and small enough to be put in a breast pocket. It seemed to be a fine industrial product, the same as an actual gun. That her opponents carried guns like this was proof that she was dealing with an illegal organization. Knowing this, she could not deny that she had failed to be careful enough.

And here, when she'd heard there was a group that gathered young people with psychic powers from all over the country for education and training, she couldn't help but think of that incident of three years ago. That was why she'd taken the young people under her wing, and made up her mind to find out the truth about the facility called the Greenhouse they'd escaped from. She'd already been making preparations to do it.

But she'd lose everything if they were taken captive by the enemy now.

If the Greenhouse had anything to do with the disappearance of her colleagues three years ago, being taken would be the end of her; they'd uncover her identity in no time.

If that happened, then Hiyama-san would likely be cast from darkness into oblivion. Just like her missing colleagues.

Sweat greased the palm of the hand that held the paralyzer gun.

She'd taken some test shots into the hill behind the school to test its performance. Since it was constructed to shoot special paralyzer bullets, it could only fire three rounds at a time. There were roughly ten attackers. Even if she was able to take out three of them, she'd get hit with return fire while she was changing cartridges.

There was no way she could win.

If Xiao Long, who could take out someone from a distance, wasn't hurt . . .

She heard some voices talking urgently in the dark. It looked like the enemy was on the move. They were slowly coming to raid the shack, walking carefully so as not to make any noise. Taking aim at one, Hiyama-san took a deep breath to steady herself. She didn't know if they had the same kind of gun that she did. For the time being, she'd take out the first three. Damn the torpedoes, full speed ahead. With this in mind, she put her finger on the trigger.

"Hiyama-san, wait," came a voice suddenly.

Startled, she looked back. Two eyes looked back, shining in the darkness.

It was Jôi.

"Jôi! You're awake?" she exclaimed.

"Over there in those shadows!"

A shot rang out. All at once guns were trained on the spot where Hiyama-san and the others were.

"Tch, looks like they found us. Thanks to *you.*"

"It's okay. Please shoot just one shot, Hiyama-san. Aim at the third man from the left," said Jôi. He spoke clearly, not like someone who'd only just awakened from a long sleep.

"You just woke up. What are you saying?"

"Just do as I say. If you do, we'll be able to escape." At Jôi's confident words, Hiyama-san remembered what Ayano and the others had said about Jôi's ability.

If he really did know the future . . .

"All right. I'll try it. But I don't know how this is going to turn out." Hiyama-san trained her gun at the target Jôi had suggested.

"When I give you the sign, go ahead and pull the trigger."

Hiyama-san nodded.

"Hey! We know you're in there. Come out quietly and no one gets hurt." The man lowered his gun and approached, not knowing Hiyama-san was armed.

"Now."

At Jôi's signal, Hiyama-san pulled the trigger.

The man she had targeted was thrown over backward. Visible confusion roiled the attackers.

"I have two shots left. Can I shoot?" Hiyama-san asked Jôi, thinking that she could easily hit another two more.

Jôi said, "No, it's okay. I'll do the rest," and without hesitation, walked out into the open.

"Huh? What're you doing?!"

"Look, it's Jôi!" the Farmers shone their mag-lights on Jôi.

Still, Jôi approached them calmly and pointed at one man. "Leave. If you don't you're going to get hurt!"

"Damn kid!" The soldier aimed his paralyzer gun at Jôi and fired.

That was it. Hiyama-san looked away. At this distance, there was no way even a novice could miss.

Yet the bullet went astray.

No, Jôi had dodged it—a paralyzer bullet fired from just a foot away, just by bending his body slightly.

In the next moment, the man who had fired was struck lightly in the temple by something Jôi had in his hand and collapsed quickly.

What happened next took only a few seconds.

One after another, the men tried shooting Jôi with their guns. However, as each of the men went to shoot Jôi, they lost sight of him and each was felled by a single blow. Another one took aim and fired, but his shot was dodged easily, and he was knocked out by Jôi's counterattack, the same as the first one.

"It's no use. Retreat! Everyone fall back!"

At the command of someone who seemed to be the leader, it took fewer than ten seconds for the remaining attackers to escape.

"They're gone, Hiyama-san." With this, Jôi threw away what he'd been holding in his right hand. It was a baseball bat grip about four inches long. It rolled away with a dry sound.

How could a single strike with something as light as that knock down grown man after grown man?

Hiyama-san came out from where she had been hiding and asked agitatedly, "What was that thing you just did? How could you dodge a bullet fired from so close?

And how come tough guys like that each fell like a load of bricks when a slender guy like you hit them once lightly?"

"Because I know."

"What?"

"Because I know how to move to not get hit by a bullet, whether my opponent will miss me, and how and where to hit my opponents to make them fall down. So it's easy."

"You say . . . you know? That can't be!"

"Can't you understand?"

"Of course not. Even if you know how to do it, it's not usually like you *can* do it, right?"

"But don't these things happen sometimes? Like sometimes it'll happen that a child will fall five stories off an apartment balcony and escape without a scratch? A plane will crash and some people will live? On the other hand, it's not that unusual for people to die just by slipping and falling in the street. If you know all these coincidences and miracles in advance and choose your moves beforehand, then dodging bullets or knocking men out simply isn't that difficult. Don't you think?"

She could understand the words. Yet Hiyama-san's common sense refused to agree. Perhaps she conveyed that somehow, because Jôi looked disappointed. "You sure are stubborn. But I knew that."

"You knew that? Since when?"

"Since I woke up."

"You knew my name, too?"

"Of course," Jôi answered, smiling. It was the smile of an angel.

"Hiyama-san."

"Yeah? What?"

"Please look after Xiao Long. I have to go help my

friends." Dumbfounded, Hiyama-san watched his re-
treating form as he ran through the dark garden.

"Christ, that Kakeru sure hooked up with a bizarre
bunch of kids," she muttered to herself as she took her
mobile phone from her pocket.

She dialed the number for the police and was going
to press the "talk" button when she stopped. She didn't
know how to explain this. Was she going to say that a
bunch of young people with psychic powers were riot-
ing? That a bunch of bad men from a secret organization were shooting guns on school grounds?

They'd only laugh at her or tell her to stop pulling
pranks in the middle of the night.

And this was something that a suburban police force
wouldn't be able to deal with anyway.

Hiyama-san dialed the late-night emergency phone
number for the place where she used to work, and con-
nected to the man who used to be her boss. They'd
stayed in touch ever since she'd left, and Hiyama-san
knew for certain that he'd believe her. When he'd been
her boss, he hadn't gone easy on her just because she
was a woman. Hiyama-san had fulfilled demanding mis-
sions, and she was grateful not to have had it any other
way.

And, for a brief time, they had also been lovers.

Still, even to her boss, she decided to hide the existence of the young people with psychic powers for
now, and simply told him the fact that they were being
attacked by a dangerous underground organization.
Although he had some doubts about the situation
Hiyama-san was in, he promised to help. "I'll send some
police right away for something different. Stand by and
wait for them," he said, and hung up the phone.

"Stand by and wait for them . . . huh?"

The word *reinstatement* came to mind.

In this situation, maybe it was better for her to operate with the organization at her back.

And to clear away the disgrace of three years before.

"I can't just stay here. I wonder what's happened to Kakeru?" Hoisting the unconscious Xiao Long on her back, she set off for the school building where the psychics were doing battle.

CHAPTER 6

THE ONE-IN-A-MILLION MIRACLE

I hung in space, roughly six feet above the floor of the old wooden gym.

Using his telekinesis, Takemaru sent me flying toward the basketball hoop. I hit the headboard as fast as if I had been on a bicycle, grabbed the rim, and held on like my life depended on it.

I was lucky I'd hit the backboard with my shoulders. If I'd struck it headfirst I probably would've gotten a concussion and passed out right then and there.

Takemaru used tremendous bursts of telekinetic power to throw me in all directions, trying to tear me off from where I clung to the rim. I resisted with all my might. Takemaru must have been getting tired, too, though, because he sat down and stopped using his power.

"Tenacious, aren't you," he said, looking annoyed. "I don't know what you're up to, but the way you just hang on to that rim without using your power is just disgusting. Let's just go at it as hard as we can, Kakeru. You *do* have amazing power, don't you?"

"Well, they're not all that strong, really," I said. The truth was that I was at my limit just from the pain of holding on, but I wasn't going to let go if I didn't know when the next attack was coming.

"Are you pretending to be modest? Or do you think I'm stupid?"

"I don't think you're stupid! That's not what I meant, really."

"Well, then, use your powers! Show me! Can't you make a car crash, call up some wind, or make ten bullets all miss you?

"Humph, think you're pretty big, there, don't ya. Well, then I have an idea, too." As if he were rummaging through the contents of the gym, garbage, broken chairs, moldy old mats, and other detritus began swirling around the room. Then his eyes fell upon the vaulting horse and its stacked parts. He grinned broadly. "You can go ahead and stay there hanging on the rim as long as you want. I'm going to make this horse fly through the air and hit you. So just don't move."

Takemaru faced the broken-down, dust-covered vaulting horse and began to focus his mind. The top piece began to rattle.

"Just a sec! Wait, Takemaru!"

"What? You want to do it now?"

"It's not that. I want you to listen to what I have to say."

"What's that?"

"I want you to stop this kind of stuff. I don't know what the guys at the Greenhouse told you, but now that you've developed these amazing powers, don't you think it's silly that they use you for this kind of thing?"

"Silly?"

"There must be a better way to help people, help the world, don't you think? Right? That would be much better. I bet you'd be an instant hero. Maybe you'd even be on TV!"

"Heh heh, isn't it *you* who's being silly? You have the same power I do. You must know what the average person in this world thinks of us when they see our powers."

Nope, no idea. And I sure don't have the same power you have.

"Hey, Kakeru. If you're a psychic, you must have thought about this, too, right? I think if we showed the world our powers, maybe some people would be interested, and maybe we'd get on TV. We'll create some excitement, but so do freaks at a circus sideshow. Their interest would soon turn into fear. If we set those monsters loose, they'll think we don't know how much evil they'll do to us. They might hurt us, or put us in prison and perform experiments on us. Am I right?"

I had no answer.

He was probably right. Human beings were beasts who feared anything different. When faced with someone with supernatural powers, they might worship him like a god, or be persecuted like the devil. Or nailed to a cross by the powers that be, like Jesus, even though he was said to be the son of God.

The fact was, I honestly had to say that the first time I'd seen Ayano's power with my own eyes had been terrifying. The only reason I hadn't run away was that she'd asked me to help her.

If you're willing to count magicians who did parlor tricks like bending spoons, you'd find that throughout history both the East and the West have acknowledged the existence of psychics. But I'd never seen anyone on the TV news who had verifiable powers. But the simple truth was there could be a lot them. Maybe it was just their fear of being persecuted that drove them to desperately try to hide their powers, not make them publicly known. After all, I'd met around seven genuine psychics just in the past two days.

But supposing someone did know about their powers. Then they might get hidden away by some group of people who wanted to use them, like Ayano and the others had been. This way they'd never attract the attention of average people like us, and there would be no one to confirm their existence, even if someone did suspect the truth.

I was sure that was the reason.

Suddenly I felt very sorry for Takemaru, who had had such a hard life. For years, he had been bullied without reason, but now that he had obtained the power to overcome his situation, he had to live in fear of someone finding out about that very power.

What a sad fate. Maybe, behind the violent acts he perpetrated, was a heart crying out for help. Maybe it was crying out now, "Somebody save me . . ."

It wasn't just Takemaru. Ayano and the other three were the same. I was sure that this was the source of their incredible bond. They were friends beyond compare, living with the same fate. That's why Kaito had chosen Ayano and the others over his friends from the Nationless Quarter, who, deep down, were probably afraid of him.

"Um, Kakeru?"

I turned back to answer Takemaru's question.

"Huh? Wh-what?"

Right. If this was no time to be sympathizing with Takemaru, it was no time to be thinking about Ayano and the others, either.

"I think I like you."

"Y-you do?"

"I have a feeling we could be friends. Actually I was

planning to tear you up to prove to you how powerful I am, but I'll cut you a break if you listen to me."

"Wha-what? What do you want to say?"

"Will you come with me to the Greenhouse? And work with me to change the world? You and I are harbingers of a new wave of human evolution. If the average human is a Neanderthal, then you and I are Cro-Magnons. No, it'd be more accurate to say there's an even bigger difference. That's why they are frightened of us, and persecute us only in the safety of numbers. That's why they made the Greenhouse. That's what Ikushima-san, who pulled us in, said. He said he wanted to play a role in the evolution of mankind."

That couldn't be. He was still deluded. I didn't know what the group that had built the secret facility known as the Greenhouse was planning. But I seriously doubted that the person who had made it was a psychic.

If that was the case, no way did he want psychics to lead the world. There must be another reason they were working on Takemaru and the others.

"Kakeru, come with me. Don't hang out with Jôi and those guys. Us psychics should be leaders. God gave us the power to free the world from the rule of the lowest and the worst, where only evil people profit."

"You're wrong, Takemaru." For some reason, I was very angry. But not at Takemaru. I was angry at the people at the Greenhouse for filling him with such arrogant ideas.

"Wrong? *What's* wrong?" returned Takemaru.

I let go of the rim and dropped to the floor. There was a crack as the rotten wood of the floor split. I staggered and landed on my butt. How pathetic. It would have looked more heroic if I'd been able to land lightly on my feet.

However . . .

I wasn't afraid of Takemaru anymore. Why was this?

"You are definitely wrong. Those people at the Greenhouse are deceiving you."

"Deceiving *me*?"

"Yep. They're using you. Can't you tell?"

"Stop bullshitting me, asshole. How could they—"

"I am not bullshitting you, you poor kid. How can you not notice that they've deceived you and they're using you?"

"You feel sorry for me? Me . . . a poor kid—"

"I do feel sorry for you. They even made you and some other people who have the same kind of psychic powers you have go and do this assassin thing."

"Feel sorry . . . for me?"

"Takemaru . . ."

Suddenly Takemaru began to shake.

His eyes looked kind of funny. He was staring into space, his mouth half open.

"Takemaru, what's wrong?"

". . . kill you."

"Huh?"

"I'm gonna kill you!"

His unfocused eyes glared at me with hatred.

Uh oh.

Quickly I grabbed hold of a nearby post.

"Die!" A psychokinetic storm broke, accompanying rage.

Already close to collapse, the worn-out gym creaked under the force of the fierce psychic waves swirling about. As Takemaru attacked me with the waves, he swirled his arms around as if wielding a weapon. I desperately clung to the post to avoid being blown away, as if I were trapped in a typhoon.

"You jerk! I'm gonna kick your butt! You're gonna see how powerful I am!" Takemaru said, taking a few capsules out of his shirt pocket and popping them all in his mouth.

"I'm gonna crush you!"

He crunched up the capsules in his mouth. Maybe it hurt, because he grimaced.

In the next minute, Takemaru had changed completely. Maybe the drugs dissolved in his saliva had been absorbed all at once, because his face contorted and he blinked his eyes a lot.

His body shivered as if he felt cold, and a shrieking scream came from deep within him, *"Heeeeeeeeeeee!"*

A tornadolike wind whirled about the small gym. No, perhaps it was only psychic waves from Takemaru.

The fierce psychokinetic shock waves coming from Takemaru, much more powerful than before, smashed the windows into smithereens, tore apart the floorboards, scattered chairs all around, tossed the vaulting horse and mats in midair, and then dashed them against the walls.

The half-demolished gym, its support columns rotten, couldn't withstand this onslaught much longer.

With a crack, the top of the post I clung to broke and fell, triggering the other thick posts surrounding the floor to break one after the other.

When the first pillar fell, I was thrown close to the entrance. The door had already become unblocked.

I tumbled outside, but I soon turned around to search for Takemaru. He was on his knees holding his head. All the while, his small, frail body let off a torrent of psychic waves that were so strong they were visible.

He was out of control.

It was probably impossible for an inexperienced mind to control an explosive burst of psychokinesis brought on by drugs. His raging power knew no limits. The walls and poles of the wooden gym continued to crumble.

Finally, the gym itself started to shake slowly. I saw the shaking gradually get bigger and I had a feeling it was going to collapse, trapping Takemaru under the rubble. Without thinking, I ran back inside the gym.

"Takemaru! Get out of here!"

Desperately I charged at Takemaru, dodging the glass shards and chunks of ceiling raining down. Takemaru finally looked back over his shoulder and noticed me.

"Ah . . . ahhh . . . ooh . . ."

He approached me unsteadily, with a wordless moan, tears welling up in his eyes. He reached out. Just then . . .

Crack crack crack. With a sound like thunder, the gym came tumbling down. I reached out and grabbed Takemaru's hand. We had to get out of there.

But when I turned back I could no longer see the exit. Our way was blocked by fallen debris. At once, I looked up at the ceiling. The ceiling, which should have been thirty feet above us, was now only a few feet away. Infinite piles of rubble, broken poles, and boards rained down on top of one another. It was no use. We were going to be buried. We were going to die.

No. I'm not ready!

At that instant the inside of my head went white, and I lost consciousness, the thunderous roar of the building's collapse in my ears.

Jôi rushed to the wooden gym building where Kakeru and Takemaru had been battling just after the old building had collapsed. He inhaled some of the rising cloud of dust and choked. Covering his nose and mouth with his shirtsleeve, he forged on. Moonlight shone down on a terrible scene of rubble, smashed posts and beams, broken plaster, and galvanized iron squashed flat.

If destruction like this had occurred in a residential area, it would have resulted in a huge commotion, even in the middle of the night, but luckily this junior high school was surrounded by nothing but rice fields and woods. Before the police that Hiyama-san had called arrived, he had to do what he had to do. He thought this as he went to push his way through the rubble when . . .

"Jôi!"

"Dude, when did you wake up?!"

Ayano and Kaito ran toward him as fast as they could.

"You guys are safe?"

"Well, yeah, somehow," said Kaito. He had been hit in the face and blood trickled from the corner of his mouth. Ayano was also marked with signs of exhaustion.

"Looks like you beat Maya and Sho, but just barely." After all, Jôi couldn't read the whole future. But he had sensed that Ayano and the others would come through without being killed or captured.

Still, there was a difference between being not killed or captured and being truly safe. Jôi was frankly relieved to see his two irreplaceable friends racing toward him unhurt.

"And what about those two?" Jôi inquired about the outcome of the battle.

"I looked all over for Maya but couldn't find her. All the running around has worn me out. She must have run off," said Ayano, a little regretfully.

Kaito stepped back on his right foot. "I almost got Sho!"

"My goodness, are you sure? You're covered in blood!" said Ayano.

"Yeah? Don't be stupid. He's in worse shape. Burns all over him. But, well, I couldn't just go burn him to death, so I let him go this time."

"Well, whatever you did is okay. But Jôi, what's this?" Ayano pointed at the mountain of rubble that had once been the gym. "Where are Kakeru and Takemaru? Don't tell me the two of them did this with their psychokinesis?"

"Yep. Looks like it. The two of them are probably under all this rubble."

"What? What did you say?"

"C'mon, you're kidding! Buried alive?"

"It's all right. They're alive. They're safe," said Jôi.

"Y-you're sure?" Ayano quavered.

"I'm sure, no mistake."

"I'm so happy . . ."

"Tch. I'm shocked."

Ayano and Kaito let out big sighs of relief. Jôi said to them, "But if we don't get moving before the police get here, there'll be trouble."

"Police? Who woulda called *them*?"

"Hiyama-san, of course. Lots of them will get here any second now. That's one reason why the Farmers, Maya, and Sho have already left."

Jôi had a vague sense that the reason the enemy had retreated was not just that.

However, now was not the time to talk about it. Now was the time to build their self-confidence by working together to drive their enemies away.

"Jôi, I'll be right back. I'm going to go look for Kakeru!" No sooner were the words out of her mouth when Ayano shut her eyes and began to project herself.

Wake up!

It sounded like my mother was calling me.

I have school today? Time to get up?

Huh?

The Golden Week vacation is over already?

My mom and sisters are back from Hawaii? . . . What was it that I was doing?

Wake up, Kakeru.

Uh, uh, I want to sleep.

She was waking me up early because it takes me so long to actually get out of bed.

Just a little longer. Five minutes.

Wake up!

"Ack!" I woke up with a start. But I wasn't in bed. I was on damp earth.

That's right. I remembered.

I'd fought with Takemaru at the gym being torn down . . . and then . . . hadn't I been pinned underneath when the gym collapsed?

"You're awake now, aren't you, Kakeru?" came a voice right next to me.

I started. In the tiny bit of light coming in I could see Takemaru stretched out.

"Ta-Takemaru."

"It's okay. I'm not going to do anything. Or maybe I should say I *can't* do anything. I can only speak. I have no strength left to move."

It looked like he'd used up all of his psychokinesis when his powers had spun out of control.

"And you saved my life."

"I did?"

"Don't you remember? You came back in to save me. And then you shielded me and stopped the gym from collapsing like this with your psychokinesis, didn't you?"

At Takemaru's words, I shifted my gaze upward.

A complicated arrangement of support posts and beams formed a kind of ceiling. Broken boards and split beams were piled up in just such a way that it made a dome that had stopped stuff like roof tiles, walls, and shards of glass from raining down on us.

It looked like Takemaru and I were under the floor. There was bare dirt and there was a crawl space big enough for people to move around in. Our pathway out was blocked here and there with rubble and fallen wood, but if we went around those spots carefully, we might be able to escape.

Apparently we'd fallen down here below the floor through a hole that had been made when a fallen post had pierced it. It had helped that first we'd fallen through the floor, and then the support poles and beams stopped the boards and rubble just before they were going to fall on the two of us. It wasn't that I'd gotten lucky once again. It was a one-in-a-million miracle.

In the weak moonlight filtering down through spaces in the rubble, Takemaru said, "Your psychokinesis is amazing. Who would've thought you could stop all the tons of wreckage from the gym in just an instant? If you can do miraculous things like this, there was never any way someone like me could've taken you on. No wonder you stayed so calm. Ha ha."

"It's not like that, really I . . ." I had no power like this. Well, if I dared to say I had any power at all, this one-in-a-million miracle was my good fortune. "I was just really lucky, it's the truth."

Takemaru didn't move. Tears appeared in the corners of his eyes and overflowed. "You win, Kakeru. I'm sad about it, but a little relieved. I wonder why?"

"Takemaru!"

The truth was even he might have been afraid of his monsterlike power. Then he had been saved by his so-called enemy. I could understand that he might feel relieved. If that was the case, it might be a good idea to shut up about just having been lucky.

"Well, now what?" from Takemaru.

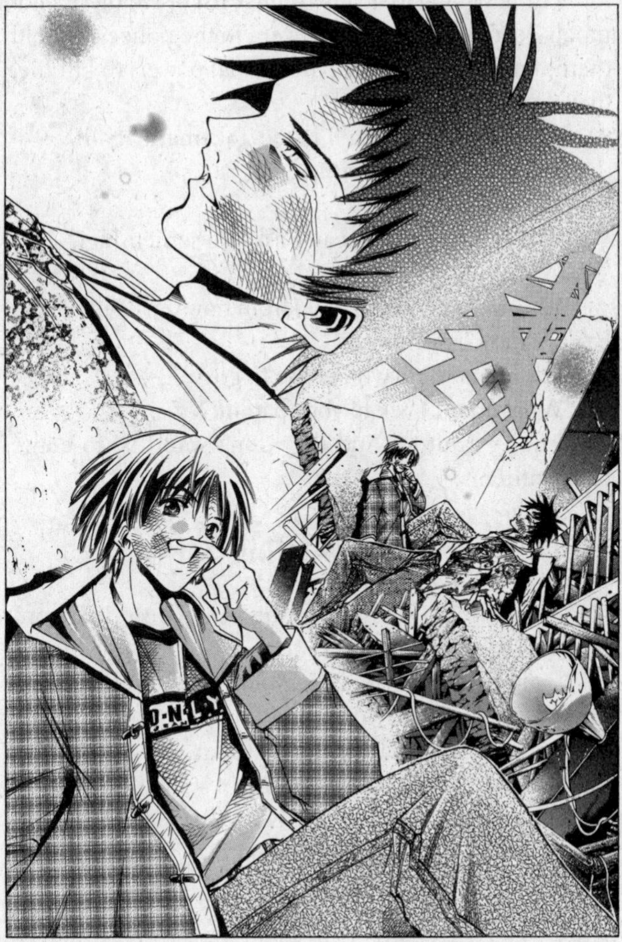
O·N·L·Y

"What d'ya mean, 'now what'?"

"I'm asking what you're going to do to me? I tried to kill you."

"I'm not going to do anything. First of all, there's not much I can do, is there." If I went to the police and told them that he tried to use paranormal powers to kill me, they'd only laugh at me.

Plus, I didn't feel like I hated Takemaru at all.

And the fight was finished.

However . . .

"Y'know, Takemaru, can I ask you something?"

"What?"

"What are you going to do from now on? Will you go back to the Greenhouse?"

"I don't have anywhere else to go."

"What about back to your parents?"

"I don't want to. And they don't want me to come back, either."

"Why?"

"They think I'm a 'poor kid' who's crazy."

What did *that* mean?

Now that you mention it, his reaction to the word *poor* was to explode in fury.

"Didn't I tell you I got sent away to a facility after I pushed the leader of the bullies onto the train tracks?"

"Uh-huh. But really, wasn't it that you didn't push him off, but how your telekinesis got started?"

"But nobody believed me. Not the station attendant, not my friends, not even my mother."

"Not even your mother?"

"My parents haven't gotten along since I was little. That was really hard and somehow I couldn't swallow my food. The doctor said I had anorexia. I got bullied and ditched at school a lot, too. I also took a few thousand dollars from the house without permission, and not just a couple of times. I caused my mom a lot of trouble . . . and I think that bully-on-the-tracks thing was the last straw."

I didn't know what to say.

"When the police came to interview me, she looked at me like I was someone she didn't know, and all she said was 'poor boy.' "

While he was talking, Takemaru sniffed, tears that he couldn't wipe away streamed down his face.

I was ready to cry, too.

But I held it in.

Stifling my tears for his sake, I said, "Y'know, I have two older sisters, and they say terrible stuff. What do you think they say?"

"I don't know . . . what?"

"They call me an all-around dork. Know what that means? It means I'm no good at sports, and I'm no good at academic stuff, either. Well, they're right. My sisters are good at both. If you want to find my class standing, it's quicker to count up from the bottom. My mom says mean stuff, too. Then she puts tons of onions in everything she cooks even though she knows I hate them. What do you think about that?"

"Your family, do they hate you?"

"I don't think they do."

"Huh?"

"I mean, when I was in elementary school, I couldn't kick myself up and over on the bars, and my second oldest sister didn't go to gymnastics practice, even though she was a big star on the team, and taught me gymnastics at the park almost every day instead. When I was studying to get into junior high school my oldest sister tutored me at home, even though she didn't get any money to do it, or anything. And she failed her own college entrance exams because of it. I felt responsible. I didn't get into any private junior highs, either. Now she'll help me study to get into high school."

It was Takemaru's turn to say nothing. He'd stopped crying and was listening to what I said.

I kept on going. "I mean, I kind of understand why my mom always wants to put onions in everything. She probably heard about it from school. That I leave leftovers from my school lunch because I won't eat onions. She says that in her generation, if someone left any food on their plate at lunch, their teacher gave them detention until they finished it. So I guess she must be worried about me, and thinks, at this rate I'll get bullied. So she's trying to get me used to them. That's gotta be it. I'm sure of it. That's right."

Takemaru gave a little smile at me for trying to convince myself through repetition.

I smiled along with him and I pointed my index finger like a clown. "Well, usually they're pretty mean. They say awful stuff about me all the time like I'm their enemy. It really gets to me. Sometimes I lose it. Not like I can do anything if I blow my stack, but y'know . . ."

Again Takemaru said nothing.

"I think that must just be how families are."

That was my true feeling.

By meeting other kids my age who had no place to go, I felt I could admit that I was an ordinary happy guy, without trying to be cool.

"Family."

"Yes. Family. Your parents are probably the same. I'm sure they haven't deserted you. A lot of stuff happened. It was probably pretty tough on your mom, too."

Silence.

"How about looking at it like that? And how about going home once to see?"

Silence. But Takemaru's tears had begun to flow.

And he had an expression on his face where I couldn't tell if he was laughing or crying.

Then, not looking at me, he said, "Kakeru . . ."

"What?"

"You're a good guy, aren't you? I knew I liked you."

"Aw, shucks. Really? Not many people say that to me. But would you please not ask me to go back with you to the Greenhouse anymore?"

"I won't. I mean, I'm not going back, either."

"Really?"

"Yeah, really. But instead . . . I want . . . what can I say? . . . I want you to be my friend," Takemaru said, bashfully.

"Of course!" I agreed, sincerely, from the bottom of my heart.

Suddenly I felt someone's presence and looked around. Ayano had projected herself out of her body and was looking at us, crying in sympathy. She'd probably come to look for us.

The sound of a police car's siren came from far away. This was a little risky. If they found us here, they'd know we were responsible for the gym getting demolished earlier than planned. Ayano made a gesture in appeal that said we'd better get out of there fast.

I nodded, and holding Takemaru in my arms because he couldn't move, I said, "Let's go. Everyone's waiting."

The person who took my hand to pull me out of the wreckage was Jôi. His smile told me he knew everything.

"Wow, Kakeru. I knew it. You are really amazing!"

Ayano hugged me like I was a puppy. It looked as if I had been misunderstood yet again.

"Tch. Dude! Outrageous!" Typical. Kaito thought I had brought the gym down, too.

"Never mind that now. Gimme a hand here," from me.

I'd dragged Takemaru. After I explained the situation to Kaito, he helped pull him out from under the floor. By that time the patrol cars had gotten close enough that we could see their red lights flashing.

"Hey, Kakeru! You're all right?" Hiyama-san came running, the unconscious Xiao Long on her back.

Now we were all together.

Since Hiyama-san was the night watchman, it was okay for her to be here, but for us, if we were found here, we'd have a lot of explaining to do. In any case, we decided to return to the janitor's room to call an ambulance for Takemaru and Xiao Long, who was still unconscious.

As we hurried back to the janitor's room, Jôi put his hand on my shoulder. "Nice to see you again, Kakeru."

I'd seen Jôi while he was asleep, but this was the first time I'd met him while he was awake. There was only that one time when he'd opened his eyes briefly where we'd seen each other.

But for some reason a feeling of nostalgia welled up inside of me.

I knew we'd met a long time ago.

Not knowing where or when that had been, I answered, "Mm hm. Nice to see you, too."

Jôi said nothing and smiled. Like a friend from long ago. It would be some time before I understood the meaning of that smile.

The dim conference room was lit by only blue light. It was said that the reason this dreary blue lighting had been chosen for this room was that it suppressed emotion, and because it further obscured the masked faces of the committee members.

For reasons of security, the Greenhouse had few windows. This made the conference room, which was windowless, extremely stuffy. Where Arata Ikushima stood in the middle, surrounded by the gazes of the members of the Masquerade Council, breathing was harder still.

"Now, Ikushima. Please tell us why the four Wild Types that escaped are still at large, and you retreated, leaving five Farmers behind."

The words carried the additional nuance of his punishment having already been decided. Ikushima, however, was sure he could get his punishment suspended.

"Yes. Firstly, we did this because the possibility of the police being called was very high."

"That is no excuse."

"I admit that." Ikushima struggled to appear calm. "But, naturally, there was another big reason."

"What is it?" The one asking was Karaki, the director. Unlike the other committee members, he was not wearing a mask.

"I feel it was best to let them swim for a while, or to put it another way, to observe their progress."

"Why?"

Director Karaki leaned forward.

"Because . . . there's a possibility that there's a Category Zero acting with the four of them. A Category Zero is essential to our plan."

There was a stir among the members of the committee.

"The influence a Category Zero has on other psychics becomes clear when one examines the influence the person with psychic powers named Jesus Christ had on the twelve apostles two thousand years ago. What do you think? Will you entrust their care to me, Ikushima-san, for a while?"

The committee members began to exchange opinions with those next to them.

Trying to hide his smile, Ikushima thought, *Look, all you greedy, masked fools. Soon you will all cry.*

Already the aspiration to overthrow the plan created by the Masquerade was budding inside of Ikushima.

A Category Zero.

Inside of Ikushima that word got bigger and bigger. However, it was still early.

What he should do now was choose a new member from among the Cultivated Types and send them in after those five.

Preparations were progressing steadily. The day drew near . . .

Five days after the ruckus at the school, I welcomed back my mom and sisters from Hawaii with an innocent look on my face.

Ayano, Kaito, Xiao Long, and Jôi all stayed with Hiyama-san, and every day the six of us took the opportunity to completely clean up all signs of our misadventure.

My mom and sisters were in high spirits, pulling bags on casters packed full of handbags and shoes from designer stores. Their present to me was a Tag Heuer diver's watch. It was an expensive souvenir, but not one I asked for or to my taste.

Well, then why did they buy it for me? I could just hear their conversation in my head.

Hey, Mom, don't you think something like this will encourage Kakeru to spend more time outdoors?

Yeah, Sis is right, we have to get him to graduate from staying in his room all the time playing with dolls.

Why, you're right. Let's get it for him. It's light and easy to take back home, after all.

I didn't think they had to worry. I was going to go out more from now on. But they'd never know the real reason why. As if they'd even believe me.

Thanks to some quick thinking by Hiyama-san, the destruction of the gym and all the broken glass in the hallway was attributed to a whirlwind that happened only in that area. That three patrol cars had come to the school and found five men with suspicious weapons unconscious near the storage shed in the garden never made it into the scandal sheets, nor was there even a school announcement about it.

If that was due to Hiyama-san's efforts, then just as I suspected, she was more than just a handyman.

Takemaru was sent to a special hospital for his state of mental lethargy. This was also owing to Hiyama-san's connections. I was sure that Takemaru would keep his promise to go back to his parents after he was discharged. His family had probably been looking for him. I was worried that the Farmers would come after him to take him back, but Jôi and the others said that they would save him if that happened.

And I would, too, of course.

Most of all, Hiyama-san was full of confidence that we didn't need to worry about Takemaru. Before we knew anything about it, Hiyama-san had done various things. There were many days that she was gone from the janitor's room, and secret-seeming calls came to her mobile phone.

I knew it. She wasn't just anybody. Who was the person called Akira Hiyama, anyway? She kept saying things like, "Next time it's *our* turn to attack." Wonder what *that* meant? Was something freaky going to happen before long?

I felt a little scared.

Incidentally, Jôi and the others all still believed I

have psychic powers. Omniscient Jôi seemed to believe this as well, which was strange.

I couldn't bring it up now, and when I secretly confessed to Hiyama-san, she said she thought it was probably okay to let them think that. And I really did save the four of them and Takemaru, so I should be proud of myself. Somehow I didn't feel that was really the problem, but whatever.

Oh, yeah, right. There was one other big piece of news: Jôi and the others transferred to my junior high school. Jôi had bought a lottery ticket that won them millions of yen, and the four of them rented a single-family home close by. Naturally, Jôi had used his prescience to buy tickets that might win. I thought it was kind of sneaky, though.

At school, Xiao Long was in seventh grade, and Jôi and Kaito were in the next class. And Ayano was in my class, sitting next to me.

Dressed in her midi-blouse and greeting students with a "Pleased to meet you," she tried to look like a typical junior high school student. The only thing not typical about her was that she was so cute that all the boys in the class cheered. Things were going to be fun, I thought, as the buzzing kept up among the boys.

"Ohh, who's that?"

"Wowee!"

A girl in a school uniform stood in the doorway.

It took one look to see why the boys had raised their voices.

She was every bit as beautiful as Ayano.

"I'm sorry to be tardy, sir," said the girl, with a bob of her head.

"Oh, there you are. We've already finished with introductions for this other student. Well, come in."

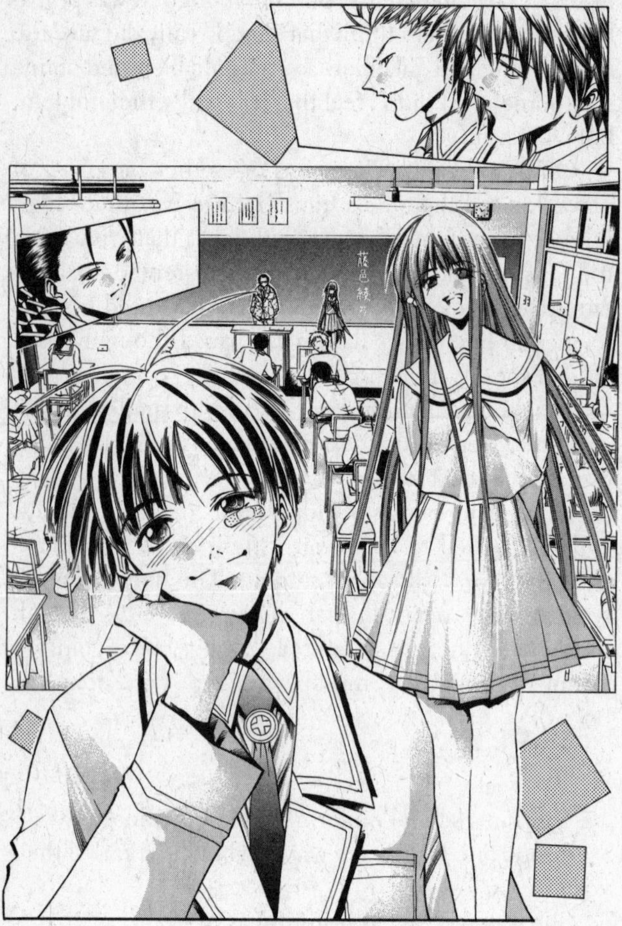
藤邑綾乃

Bowing her head again, the girl approached the podium.

It looked like Ayano wasn't the only new student joining the class.

Actually, in addition, there were new students in Jôi and Kaito's class, too, as well as in all the other classes.

Little did I know then that these boys and girls, who came one after the other to our peaceful school in the countryside, would lure us into another nightmare.

Pleased to meet you, readers. My name is Yuya Aoki.

Well, if you've read the manga *Get Backers*, then this is probably not the first time you've picked up one of my works. But this should be the first time you've read a novel I've written under the name Yuya Aoki (although I've actually written a number of novels under different names).

I consider my true vocation to be that of manga scriptwriter. But I'd like to talk a little about why this time I wrote a novel, and not a manga.

Have any of you been asked by your teacher or your parents to read a *real* book, not manga, once in a while? I heard that a lot as a child. Actually, I read a lot of novels, too, but I feel like my parents only disapproved when it was manga they saw me reading. But not in the least discouraged, I went right on reading them, and finally, after being told harshly not to read them, I decided to make creating stories for manga my job.

Even when I think about it now, all the manga I read was preparation for my future profession.

And, all joking aside, there are really so many things I learned from the manga I read as a child. They are still useful now, and I remember them well enough to surprise people I talk to. I'm sure it's because I eagerly read my favorite manga over and over again. They say that the things one learns by forced studying are entered into the temporal lobe and are then quickly forgotten, but that knowledge pleasurably obtained is stored in the frontal lobe and is not so easy to forget. Basically, the trick to increasing the knowledge you retain as an adult is to choose interesting reading material, be it manga or anything else.

But I digress. Let us return to the main point.

Since I write both manga and novels, I realize that making a sustained comparison between manga and novels, asking which one is better, more interesting, and more educational, and which is lacking in quality, dull, and frivolous, is completely pointless. Both have distinctive methods of expression, each with its own advantages, and both have a charm that one would not want to do without. From the writer's point of view, no book is interesting or boring or educational or frivolous just because it's manga, or just because it's a novel. Please judge books, not by their medium, but by the quality of their workmanship, and the execution of the author's intentions.

By no means read them with the feeling that, in manga, the treatment of the characters can be superficial, or that it's all right for a novel to be difficult and dull. Both should be written with the aim of having characters that are engaging and stories that are easy and interesting to read.

So why is it that so many young people dislike novels? Two reasons have occurred to me.

One is that there are still not many novels that are easy for you young people to read. I cannot disagree that the difficult writing and sophisticated worldview found in novels for adults is hard going for young people who are just getting their start reading.

Reason number two (actually, this is the more important reason), is that it's just that young readers are unaccustomed to reading novels.

For example, in the case of playing games on TV, it wasn't any fun until you got used to that controller, was it? It's the same thing. But once you get good at games, they're fun, aren't they?

In the same way, novels can also be fun. However, since there are no pictures to tell the story as there are in manga, the imagination needs to be fueled by the words.

Stick with it and read through it. Young people should soon get the hang of it.

Above all, I tried to make *Psycho Busters* as much like a manga as I could. I tried playing with the characters as I pleased, making them mangalike; drawn like manga, with the challenge of choosing a mangalike theme. I took a chance in dropping the idea of creating a difficult and complicated work, and instead tried putting in scenes where the exchange between characters would make people laugh or cry a bit.

Make this work your harbor from which to row out into the limitless, vast, stormy, dramatic ocean of entertainment known as novels. And I want you to cultivate your imagination—after all, young people have incredible imaginations.

This is why I spun my story in the shape of a novel.

The first volume is a prologue to a story of great adventure. It's going to become more and more interesting, and that is truly how I want it to be. I hope you enjoy it.

Yuya Aoki

Born in Tokyo in 1962, the versatile **Yuya Aoki** has won acclaim and popularity in Japan for his work in manga, prose fiction, and television. He is best known in the United States for the smash hit manga series *Get Backers*.

Rando Ayamine was born in Japan's Hyogo prefecture in 1974. After graduating from the Tokyo Animation Institute, he became the assistant to Fujisawa Toru, the famed creator of *GTO*. He first headlined his own manga series with *Get Backers*, created in collaboration with Yuya Aoki.